Building Structures with Young Children

Trainer's Guide

THE YOUNG SCIENTIST SERIES

Trainer's Guide

building
structures
with
young
children

The
*Young
Scientist*
Series

Ingrid Chalufour and Karen Worth
Education Development Center, Inc.

Redleaf Press®
www.redleafpress.org
800-423-8309

Published by Redleaf Press
10 Yorkton Court
St. Paul, MN 55117
www.redleafpress.org

Written by Ingrid Chalufour and Karen Worth, with Robin Moriarty, Jeffrey Winokur, and Sharon Grollman

Cover and interior design by Percolator
Interior typeset in Weiss
Printed in the United States of America
16 15 14 13 12 11 10 09   5 6 7 8 9 10 11 12

This book was written with the support of National Science Foundation Grant ESI-9818737. However, any opinions, findings, conclusions, and/or recommendations herein are those of the authors and do not necessarily reflect the views of NSF.

ISBN 978-1-929610-51-8

Printed on acid-free paper

The Young Scientist series was developed by a team of early childhood and science educators from the Tool Kit for Early Childhood Science Education project at Education Development Center, Inc. (EDC) and was funded by a grant from the National Science Foundation. The project was led by Ingrid Chalufour from the Center for Children and Families and Karen Worth from the Center for Science Education. Listed below are the key members of the team, all of whom contributed substantially to the work from its conceptualization to the final product.

INGRID CHALUFOUR has designed and conducted professional development programs for staff in child care programs, Head Start, public schools, and social service agencies for more than thirty-five years.

SHARON GROLLMAN, a senior research associate at EDC's Center for Children and Families, has developed educational materials for more than twenty years. Prior to coming to EDC, she was part of a research team in early childhood.

ROBIN MORIARTY is a research associate at EDC's Center for Science Education. Her work includes curriculum development, leading professional development programs, and working with early childhood centers. She taught young children in the Boston area for fourteen years before she joined EDC.

JEFFREY WINOKUR is a senior research associate at EDC's Center for Science Education. His work includes curriculum development and leading professional development programs for early childhood and elementary science education. He has worked in early childhood and science education for over twenty years and is an instructor in education at Wheelock College.

KAREN WORTH is a senior scientist at EDC's Center for Science Education. Her work includes the development of science curriculum and professional development programs, as well as consultation in science education for young children. She is also a graduate-level instructor at Wheelock College in the early childhood education department and has worked in the field of science and early childhood education for the past thirty-five years.

contents

acknowledgments

The Young Scientist Series was developed by the project staff of the Tool Kit for Early Childhood Science Education housed at Education Development Center, Inc. (EDC), with funding from the National Science Foundation.

Numerous educators and consultants contributed to the development and field testing of the series. We would like to thank the following people for their contributions to this work.

DEVELOPMENT TEACHERS

Cindy Hoisington
Lucia McAlpin
Carole Moyer
Rebecca Palacios
Susan Steinsick

PILOT TEACHERS

Colette Auguste
Liana Bond
Imelda DeCosta
Marlene Dure
Frank Greene
Karen Hoppe
Terry Küchenmeister
Stuart Lui
Maureen McIntee
Susan Miller
Katherine O'Leary
Carolyn Robinson
Ellen Sulek
Laurie Wormstead
Tiffany Young

FIELD TEST SITES

Bainbridge Island Child Care
    Centers, Bainbridge Island, WA
Barre Town School, Barre, VT
Berlin Elementary School,
    Berlin, VT
Blackwater Community School,
    Coolidge, AZ
Blue Hill Avenue Early Education
    Center, Boston, MA

Bright Horizons at Preston
    Corners, Cary, NC
Childspace Day Care Centers,
    Philadelphia, PA
City of Phoenix Head Start,
    Phoenix, AZ
Cisco Family Connection Bright
    Horizons, Milpitas, CA
East Montpelier Elementary
    School, East Montpelier, VT
Epic Head Start, Yakima, WA
Fort Worth Museum of Science
    and History, Fort Worth, TX
Four Corners School, East
    Montpelier, VT
K–5 Inquiry-Based Science
    Program, Seattle Public
    Schools, WA
Louisiana Tech University Early
    Childhood Education Center,
    Ruston, LA
Motorola Childcare and Education
    Center, Schaumburg, IL
Pasadena Unified School District,
    Pasadena, CA
Phoenix Head Start, Phoenix, AZ
Portage Private Industry Council
    Head Start, Ravenna, OH
School for Early Learning, Spring
    Branch Independent School
    District, Houston, TX
Thomson Early Childhood Center,
    Seattle, WA
UMC Child Development Lab,
    Columbia, MO

Valle Imperial Project in Science,
    El Centro, CA
William H. Rowe School,
    Yarmouth, ME
Young Achievers Science and
    Mathematics Pilot School,
    Boston, MA

ADVISORY BOARD MEMBERS

Douglas Clements
David Dickinson
George Forman
Linda French
Marilou Hyson
Stephanie Johnson
Diane Levin
Mary Jane Moran
Carolyn Vieria
Sandra Williams
Diane Willow

CONSULTANTS

Mary Eisenberg
Pat Fitzsimmons
Ben Mardell
Janet Sebell

We also would like to acknowledge
the following people at EDC:

Erica Fields, Research Assistant
Kerry Ouellet, Editor and
    Production Manager
Susan Weinberg, Senior
    Administrative Assistant

introduction

"The Young Scientist professional development materials were very, very helpful. As an instructor I knew just what to do and the teachers really enjoyed the workshops. I feel their excitement has transferred to the children. Both boys and girls are interested in and excited about their science explorations."

—EARLY CARE AND EDUCATION PROGRAM DIRECTOR

Cindy Richards, director of the West Side Early Childhood Center, found that the current trends toward standards and child outcomes caused her to question what children were really learning. Teachers were concentrating on helping children to recognize letters, rather than encouraging children to look at books or use print to communicate their own ideas. Her teachers would set up a science table, but children rarely spent time there or investigated a topic in-depth. Ms. Richards had been sending teachers to workshops for years—hoping her teachers would learn new strategies for improving early literacy, science, and math—but the effects were rarely apparent in the classroom. Ms. Richards felt the time had come to change her approach but she was unsure what she could do to improve teaching and learning in her program.

Then she was asked if her program would field-test the Young Scientist teacher guides—on water, living things, and structures—and the accompanying professional development program. Ms. Richards was reluctant at first, wondering if this was just one more gimmick, just one more shot in the dark. Flipping through the materials, she was surprised to see how extensive the program was—which was a bit daunting. But she hoped its comprehensive nature might lead to the changes she was looking for. So she said yes. She found that the hands-on exploration built teachers' understanding of the science content, inquiry process, and the Young Scientist approach to teaching. The video vignettes helped teachers connect this content approach to their own teaching practice. Ms. Richards notes, "One of the most important things I learned was the importance of time. It takes time to learn new approaches and integrate them into teaching practice. It takes time to provide teachers with the ongoing support they need to sustain successful change." As a result of participating in this professional development program, Ms. Richards sees evidence of teachers applying what they have learned. Teachers are engaging children in in-depth science explorations over time. Teachers' conversations with children don't just focus on management now (such as "Make sure to put the blocks away when you're done"), but on what children are doing and thinking (such as "How could you make the building stronger?"). For the first time, many teachers are documenting children's observations and ideas and using them to extend learning. This has been evident not only in science, but in other domains as well. Ms. Richards reflects, "Teachers see their role, their curriculum, and the children in a new way. For the first time, they are recognizing and capitalizing on the science in the everyday, which helps them to guide children's science learning more effectively. At the same time, they appreciate what children notice and wonder about, what they can do, and understand."

Others who have field-tested the Young Scientist series have had similar reactions:

"I found it really easy to follow. Everything was very clear. Anybody could use it. The teachers didn't lose interest. They really liked the hands-on parts, and they were very engaged in the reflective discussions."
—**PUBLIC SCHOOL ADMINISTRATOR**

"When I read through the workshops, they looked so good, I decided we needed to do them all!"
—**HEAD START DIRECTOR**

The Young Scientist

The above vignette suggests the excitement that can be generated when teachers really enjoy learning about and trying out new teaching approaches. In order to build the knowledge and skills teachers need to implement an inquiry-based science curriculum, the Young Scientist provides both teacher guides and a comprehensive set of training materials for each of three science explorations:

- *Discovering Nature with Young Children* invites children to assume the role of a naturalist as they observe and learn about plants and animals in the immediate outdoors, as well as in their own classrooms.
- *Exploring Water with Young Children* helps children examine the properties of water.
- *Building Structures with Young Children* engages children in investigating the relationships between building materials and design and the strength and stability of the structures.

DEVELOPMENT AND TESTING

The Young Scientist is a result of a four-year grant funded by the National Science Foundation. It draws on current understanding of best practice in science teaching and learning. Key to the development process has been the involvement of practitioners and experts from the field who have helped us design our approach, review draft documents, and test the curriculum and professional development materials. The final stage in this process was a national field test conducted in 2001 and 2002, in nineteen early childhood programs including Head Start, pre-K, child care centers, and private nursery schools. Program directors, education managers, and curriculum coordinators from these programs planned and implemented the training activities. Ninety teachers participated in the workshops and used the teacher's guides in their classrooms. Results revealed that some combination of the workshops and more informal support was important to help teachers apply their new learning in the classroom. Moreover, participants reported evidence of science learning in children's questions, observations, and discussions.

Overview of the Trainer's Guide

Teachers often feel insecure and inadequate about their own understanding of science concepts and do not realize how they can learn through inquiry and then use their new understanding in the classroom. These training materials focus on helping teachers begin to gain an understanding of the underlying science concepts in the *Building Structures with Young Children* teacher's guide and learn to use that guide to facilitate children's inquiry.

This guide includes all of the instructions, print, and video materials you will need to provide rich professional development experiences for your teachers as they implement the *Building Structures with Young Children* teacher's guide in their classrooms. When workshops and guided discussions are combined with mentoring over time, your training program will lead to a quality science education program.

The trainer's guide has four components:

- A set of six **BASIC WORKSHOPS:** These workshops use hands-on experiences and reflective conversations to provide teachers with a practical understanding of the science content and inquiry process that will inform their teaching; help in recognizing the science in children's work; and help in guiding children's explorations. These workshops also provide an overview of all sections of the teacher's guide.

- Eight **ADVANCED WORKSHOPS:** These workshops use samples of children's work and conversations to help teachers build a practical understanding of their multifaceted role as facilitators of science inquiry.

- A structure for **GUIDED DISCUSSIONS:** These discussions provide a forum for small groups of teachers to use classroom documentation to stimulate collaborative reflection on their own science teaching and plan new and more effective approaches.

- A description of a **MENTORING PROGRAM:** This section helps mentors use classroom observations and conferencing to support teachers with their individual challenges and help them assess their teaching and refine their practice.

The following sections will help you plan and implement your program:

- **PLANNING AN EFFECTIVE PROFESSIONAL DEVELOPMENT PROGRAM** (below) will help you select the appropriate components and schedule your events.

- **GETTING STARTED** (p. 6) describes a three-step process for preparing yourself for conducting the basic and advanced workshops.

- **RESOURCES** (p. 193) offers a range of tools, including descriptions of each of the instructional strategies used in the workshops, guidance and forms for evaluating teacher growth and planning guided discussions, a log of the video vignettes, and a bibliography for you and for teachers.

Planning an Effective Professional Development Program

These comprehensive training materials, designed to support teacher implementation of the *Building Structures with Young Children* teacher guide, can be adapted to the needs of your particular program and teachers. We suggest you plan a three-stage program:

1. Help teachers become familiar with the teacher's guide and the science concepts and inquiry process at the heart of *Building Structures with Young Children*.

2. Help teachers build their capacity as inquiry-based science teachers.

3. Sustain progress you have made and support teachers as they continue to refine their science teaching practice.

Implement these stages one at a time, based on your assessment of teachers' strengths and needs.

STAGE 1: LEARN TO USE THE TEACHER'S GUIDE

Use the six basic workshops to help teachers understand the building structures science concepts, the inquiry process, and the teacher's guide. These workshops, which consist of one three-hour introduction and five one-and-a-half-hour sessions, provide the knowledge and experience teachers need as they begin to implement the teacher's guide. When scheduling the workshops consider several factors:

- Teachers will need the first three workshops before they begin using *Building Structures with Young Children*. These workshops will introduce the science concepts and the nature of science inquiry, help them prepare their environment, and provide an overview of open exploration.

- Teachers will need workshops 4 and 5 before moving on to focused exploration. These two workshops will provide a hands-on focused exploration and an overview of the purpose and teacher role in this stage of the exploration, preparing them to facilitate deeper investigations. Try not to wait more than three weeks between workshop 3 and 4. Teachers will need to understand how to deepen children's investigation and apply this in the classroom, otherwise the children will lose interest.

- Find ways to keep this focus on science teaching and learning in the foreground of your program's activity. Check in with teachers regularly to see how things are going in their classrooms. Do they have the materials they need? Are they finding enough time for exploration and science talks? Are the children engaged? Use mentoring or guided discussions to maintain the focus if there are extended periods between the workshops.

PROGRAM SAMPLE SCHEDULES

1. The teachers in this program were able to schedule most of their training sessions during naptime when they would otherwise be planning. They were also able to fit in a full-day session before the school year began. The director wanted to provide individual support from the beginning by scheduling two observation and conferencing sessions with each teacher during stage 1. The first helped teachers make the transition to focused exploration. The second supported their efforts to integrate representation and science talks into their regular routine and to use them effectively for science learning.

SCIENCE EXPLORATIONS WORKSHOP SCHEDULE

September 3
9:00 A.M.–3:00 P.M.
Workshops 1 and 2: Introduction and
Getting Ready

September 12
1:30–3:00 P.M.
Workshop 3: Open Exploration

Observation and conferences will be scheduled with each classroom from September 26
through October 10.

October 3
1:30–3:00 P.M.
Workshop 4: Focused Exploration of Towers

October 10
1:30–3:00 P.M.
Workshop 5: Focused Exploration

Observation and conferences will be scheduled with each teacher from October 10
through November 7.

November 7
1:00–2:30 P.M.
Workshop 6: Focused Exploration of
Enclosures

2. In another center there is no time during the day for workshops, but the teachers were eager to implement the program in their classrooms. The director offered pizza dinner and babysitting in exchange for their participation after the center closed. The director did her first observation and conference at the end of the series to help her prepare for stage 2.

HIGHLAND CHILD CARE CENTER'S SCIENCE EXPLORATIONS WORKSHOPS

Everybody Attend!!!
Pizza served at 6:30 P.M.
Workshops begin promptly at 7:00 P.M.

September 4*, 11, 18; October 9, 16; and November 13

*Note: The September 4 workshop is 6:00–9:00 P.M.

STAGE 2: BUILD CAPACITY AS INQUIRY-BASED SCIENCE TEACHERS

If you have completed the basic workshops, teachers should be beginning to use the guide and this approach to engaging children in building structures. Use "Assessing Teacher Growth" (in "Resources," p. 204) to assess their practice. Work with teachers to identify appropriate goals. "Science Teacher Development Plan" ("Resources," p. 212) is a useful resource when you are considering next steps and the level of support to provide. Teachers still at the beginning stage might need some help, individually or in a small group, with the goals that best meet their needs. The chapters on mentoring and guided discussion will help you plan your work with them.

Many teachers will be ready to move onto the advanced workshops after completing the basic ones. As you plan consider the following:

- Start with the first workshop, "Creating a Culture of Inquiry About Building Structures," which includes an individual needs assessment that will help you better understand how the teachers perceive their needs and interests.

- Plan a sequence of workshops that best reflects the needs and interests identified by them and you.

- Allow time in between workshops (at least one month) for teachers to implement the approaches presented.

- Use mentoring or guided discussions to support teachers' efforts in between the workshops.

STAGE 3: PROVIDE ONGOING SUPPORT AS TEACHERS REFINE THEIR PRACTICE

If you have not used guided discussions and mentoring before completing the basic and advanced workshops, now is the time. Regular opportunities to talk about science teaching and learning will be key to sustaining and building on the gains you have made. Guided discussions provide a vehicle for encouraging documentation and analysis of the teaching and learning going on in your program. At the same time, you will be encouraging teacher collaboration and providing a vehicle for analysis and refining science teaching. Mentoring is also an important way to help teachers progress by addressing their interests and concerns directly in relation to their classroom. Use the chapters on guided discussion and mentoring to plan this stage of your professional development program.

Getting Started

The time you spend preparing will contribute to the success of your professional development events. Here we describe the special things you can do to prepare for the workshops. Follow these steps as you get ready:

1. Become familiar with the teacher's and trainer's guides.

2. Find a location for the workshops.

3. Prepare to be an instructor.

STEP 1: BECOME FAMILIAR WITH THE TEACHER'S AND TRAINER'S GUIDES

A clear understanding of the curriculum and its science content will be essential if you are to help others understand this approach to teaching and learning. Carefully read the teacher's guide, familiarizing yourself with its approach and structure. Consider what aspects of this approach will be familiar to teachers and which ones will be new. Identify the parts of the guide that will be particularly helpful to teachers. Reading the guide more than once will help you build your own understanding of this teaching method and the various ways the guide supports teacher adoption.

Next, familiarize yourself with these professional development materials. Quickly reading the whole package will give you the big picture—an overview of the structure and content of the instructions and the supporting materials. In a more focused read, examine each aspect of the instructional approach and anticipate how teachers might respond.

STEP 2: FIND A LOCATION FOR THE WORKSHOPS

Select sites for your workshops that will be comfortable and provide good table or floor surfaces for building structures.

Round or rectangular tables will provide a good surface for the building activities in the basic workshops. Easy availability of an overhead projector, screen, VCR, and monitor will make your work easier.

STEP 3: PREPARE TO BE AN INSTRUCTOR

Familiarity with both content and process of the workshops will give you confidence as a presenter. Take the time to complete these tasks.

- Explore the building materials using the guidance in basic workshop 1 and in the "Getting Ready" section of the teacher's guide (p. 13). In addition, do the hands-on activities that are described in basic workshops 4 and 6.

- Think through the discussion questions, answering them for yourself. Try to anticipate how teachers will react and then imagine your responses.

- Preview the video vignettes that you will be showing. As you watch, think about the purpose of the vignettes, children's engagement with science, the science teaching strategies they illustrate, and what you want teachers to gain from the viewing and conversation.

- Collect the materials. You will need a variety of building materials to facilitate the explorations. Look for varied shapes, textures, and weights. Review this list early (see the section on advance preparation for each workshop) and make plans for how you will get all of these things before the day of the workshop. Suggestions for finding many of these items can be found in the "Resources" section in the teacher's guide (p. 79).

- Prepare the handouts and overheads. For the most part, you will refer participants to resources in the teacher's guide, but there are a few handouts in the professional development package that provide guidance for small group work or observation of videos. These handouts appear at the end of the instructions for each workshop. Each participant will need a copy of each handout. The final handout is an evaluation that all participants should complete at the end of the basic or advanced workshops. The overheads, found at the end of both workshop sections, give the participants a visual aid to the content. You will need to copy them onto transparencies.

- Consider how you want to handle the "Read and Reflect" preassignments, which have been included for each of the basic workshops. You will need to copy and distribute them to teachers at least a week before each session. These assignments include readings in the teacher's guide and reflection questions. Completing the assignments will ensure that teachers are familiar with the content of each session and ready to participate fully in the discussions. You will probably want to collect teachers' responses and review their reflections to gain insight into teachers' understandings. This will help you tailor sessions to meet the needs of individual teachers.

- Review key instructional strategies in the resources, which will help you effectively use the various teaching strategies in these workshops.

basic workshops

The six workshops are designed to familiarize teachers with the teacher's guide and the underlying science content. They include the following:

- Workshop 1: Introduction to *Building Structures with Young Children*—Teachers learn about the science content and inquiry skills at the heart of *Building Structures with Young Children*.

- Workshop 2: Getting Ready—Teachers prepare a science-rich environment for children's building investigations.

- Workshop 3: Overview of Open Exploration—Teachers are introduced to the purpose and flow of open exploration.

- Workshop 4: Focused Exploration of Towers—Teachers deepen their understanding of key science concepts and inquiry skills, as well as their approach to teaching and learning, through a hands-on exploration of building towers.

- Workshop 5: Overview of Focused Exploration—Teachers are introduced to the purpose and flow of focused exploration, and share their own classroom observations.

- Workshop 6: Focused Exploration of Enclosures—Teachers address the challenges of building enclosures, and further their understanding of the science and this approach to teaching.

Each workshop includes the following sections:

- At a Glance—purpose, activities, timeline, materials, and preassignment for each session
- Objectives—what you want teachers to gain by the end of the session
- Overview—activity descriptions and suggestions for time management
- Instructor Preparation—materials needed and steps to take to get ready for each session
- Detailed step-by-step instructions
- Handouts to copy for each teacher
- Overheads to copy as transparencies before each session
- "Read and Reflect" preassignments to copy and distribute at least a week before each session

You can also refer to the key instructional strategies in "Resources" (see p. 193) to help you prepare and conduct the basic workshops.

Introduction to
Building Structures with Young Children

AT A GLANCE

Purpose:
- Gain a beginning understanding of an inquiry-based approach to science teaching and learning in the early childhood classroom.
- Begin to understand the science concepts and inquiry skills central to *Building Structures with Young Children*.
- Learn about the teacher's guide and how it is organized.

Activity	Time	Materials
Introduction Introduce teachers to the basic workshops and the teacher's guide. Use a video vignette to show the program "in action." Invite teachers to share previous experiences with building.	45 minutes	• Handouts: agenda, "Read and Reflect 1" • Copies of *Building Structures with Young Children* teacher's guides • Self-adhesive note pads • VCR, monitor, and video cued to vignette 1 • Overhead projector, screen, and overhead 1.1
Building Exploration Facilitate an open exploration of building. Model the role that teachers will play with children by encouraging engagement and focusing on characteristics of the materials and design strategies.	1 hour 10 minutes	• Building materials • Books about building • Posters or pictures of buildings • Charts: "Characteristics of Building Materials," "What I Might Try to Build," and "What We Learned about Building Structures" • Camera and film or digital camera (optional)
The Science Introduce the science concepts and inquiry process, and help teachers connect them to their own building experiences.	55 minutes	• Overhead projector, screen, and overheads 1.2 and 1.3 • Copies of "Read and Reflect 2"

Preassignment: Read introduction to *Building Structures with Young Children* and excerpts from a teacher's journal, and respond to reflection questions.

Basic Workshop 1: Introduction

OBJECTIVES

- Gain beginning understanding of this approach to teaching and learning in the early childhood classroom.

- Begin to understand the science concepts and inquiry skills.

- Learn about the teacher's guide and how it is organized.

OVERVIEW

- Introduction (45 minutes)

- Building exploration (1 hour and 10 minutes)

- The science (55 minutes)

INSTRUCTOR PREPARATION

- **DISTRIBUTE "READ AND REFLECT 1"** with the teacher's guide at least one week before the workshop. Ask teachers to complete the assignment before the first workshop.

- **PREPARE AN AGENDA** that outlines the six basic workshops, as well as where and when they will take place.

- **SELECT AND SET UP** a classroom for teachers to explore. Select a classroom that has a well-equipped block area and space for exploring other building materials either at tables or on the floor. This is an opportunity to introduce building materials as you would expect teachers to do in their own classrooms. If you cannot use a classroom, try to replicate the classroom environment ensuring enough space for your teachers to work with a variety of building materials in groups of three or four. You may want to post pictures of buildings and place books about building around the areas where teachers will work.

- **REVIEW STEP 1 OF OPEN EXPLORATION** in the teacher's guide in preparation for facilitating the exploration. The exploration will model the approach described in this step.

- **PREVIEW VIDEO VIGNETTE 1.** As you look at the video find the teacher and child actions that exemplify the points you want to make about this approach. The instructions that follow provide suggestions.

MATERIALS

- Handouts: agenda, "Read and Reflect" 1 and 2

- *Building Structures with Young Children* teacher's guides for each teacher

- Building materials (at least four different types and enough for groups of three or four to have a large quantity), such as unit blocks, small-scale table blocks (such as Kapla, Dr. Drew, or miniature unit blocks), foam blocks, recycled materials (such as empty boxes, toilet paper tubes, assorted wood scraps), and straws and connectors

- Books about building

- Posters or pictures of buildings

- Small self-adhesive note pads for each teacher
- Charts: "Characteristics of Building Materials," "What I Might Try to Build," and "What We Learned about Building Structures"
- Camera and film or digital camera (optional)
- Overhead projector, screen, and overheads 1.1–1.3
- Video cued to vignette 1, VCR, and monitor

Activity

INTRODUCTION (45 MINUTES)

PURPOSE:

- To set the stage by introducing the curriculum, its vision for science teaching and learning, and the nature of the work teachers will be doing with you during the workshops
- To uncover what teachers already know about structures and the kinds of building experiences they have had, strengthening their confidence as builders

1. **GIVE A SHORT PRESENTATION** (5 minutes) that provides the teachers with a brief overview of the workshops. Distribute the agenda and review it with the teachers, being explicit about any requirements for their participation in the workshops and use of the curriculum. Tell them they will be learning the following:

   - How to use *Building Structures with Young Children* teacher's guide to explore building structures over time with children

   - Science concepts and inquiry skills intrinsic to building structures

   - The teacher's role in facilitating children's inquiry and science learning

2. **INTRODUCE THE TEACHER'S GUIDE AND THE "READ AND REFLECT" ASSIGNMENTS** (10 minutes). Tell teachers that the guide provides information and direction for conducting an investigation of building structures that can take place over several months. Mention that the read and reflect assignments are meant to introduce them to the teacher's guide and can be used to prepare for each workshop. Explain that you will refer them back to sections of the guide during the session and suggest that they use the self-adhesive notes to mark pages that are discussed for easy reference.

3. **USE VIGNETTE 1 TO INTRODUCE *BUILDING STRUCTURES WITH YOUNG CHILDREN*** (30 minutes).

   a. Begin by using overhead 1.1 to review the guiding principles listed in the introduction. Suggest that teachers look for these things as they watch the video.

OVERHEAD 1.1: *BUILDING STRUCTURES WITH YOUNG CHILDREN* **GUIDING PRINCIPLES**

- All three- to five-year-olds can successfully experience rich, in-depth scientific inquiry.

- The science content draws from children's experiences, is interesting and engaging, and can be explored directly and deeply over time.

- Expectations are developmentally appropriate; that is, they are realistic and can be tailored to the strengths, interests, and needs of individual children.

- Discussion, expression, and representation are critical ways in which children reflect on and develop theories from their active work.

- Children learn from one another.

- Teachers take on specific roles to actively support and guide children's science learning.

---

b. Introduce the vignette by saying that one Head Start classroom and two kindergartens, all from Boston, are shown. The children are all three-, four-, and five-year olds, and are engaged in a building exploration. The sequences show varied points in time, in both open and focused exploration.

c. Ask for reactions using these questions: "Did you see anything that reminded you of a guiding principle? What did you see and which principle did it exemplify?" You might also want to discuss how the teachers in the vignette compare to teachers A, B, and C in the introduction to the teacher's guide. Ask for specifics.

Make these points about the vignette and this approach to teaching and learning:

- The children seem engaged and excited about building.

- Children are able to engage at varied levels of ability.

- Representation and conversation provide important opportunities to reflect and draw meaning from building experiences.

- The teacher is key in the process of engaging in inquiry and using experiences to gain a deeper understanding of science ideas.

When discussing how the teachers in the vignette compare to teacher C, be sure to highlight the following:

- They are building on children's interest in constructive and dramatic play with blocks.

- Hands-on experiences combined with dialogue and representation promote learning key science concepts.

- They use carefully selected building materials that will provide experience with physical forces and challenge children to consider the characteristics of materials and elements of design that are important to gaining stability and balance.

- The teacher's guide inquiry, bringing children's questions forward, encouraging close observation and representation, and helping with data collection and analysis.

d. Discuss teachers' previous experiences with building for about ten minutes to help them understand the science that is intrinsic to building. Encourage a few people to talk about experiences they have had that focused on building. You might want to start the conversation by sharing a brief story of your own and then asking some questions. If you do tell a story of your own, choose one to which you think teachers can relate, one that might help them make connections to their own life.

Use the following questions to guide the discussion:

- What kinds of building experiences have you had?

- What kinds of materials did you use? How did they stay together?

- What do you think is important to do to make structures strong and stable?

- Have you ever wondered about buildings, such as why skyscrapers don't fall over?

It is important for learners to talk about what they already know. Making the connections to their knowledge and past experiences recognizes their value and helps them integrate new information. In this case, it can ease them into science by helping them realize science is already a part of their lives.

Many people have had experiences building real structures and teachers can likely remember those early times when they wanted to build with anything they could get their hands on. Some might have built with found materials such as sticks and stones, sand, empty boxes, or scraps of wood. Others might recall creating a playhouse from a refrigerator box, making a birdhouse, or building a bookshelf. Some might have built a bookcase at home or furniture for the classroom, or assembled a bed or cabinet. And still others might have worked with an architect or contractor when their house or classroom was being built.

BUILDING EXPLORATION (1 HOUR 10 MINUTES)

PURPOSE: Through the process of engaging teachers in a building exploration you will achieve the following:

- Provide a beginning experience with inquiry and the science content on which you will build throughout the workshops

- Reinforce the importance of having firsthand experience with building materials

- Model the teacher's role in facilitating scientific explorations

- Model a science talk that helps teachers build on one another's understanding in the same way children can

1. **INTRODUCE THE BUILDING EXPLORATION WITH A CHART** (10 minutes) by saying that they will be engaging in an exploration of the kind they will facilitate for children—however, this particular experience is designed for adults. Begin the exploration by showing teachers each material they will be building with and letting them feel them. Ask the group what kinds of structures they might build with each material and why (such as solid, heavy blocks are good for strong towers; straws and connectors are good for tall, airy constructions). Try to keep the discussion focused on the differences of the materials and how those differences might affect building with them. List people's responses on the chart, "Characteristics of Building Materials."

Ask a few questions, such as the following:

- What do you think are some challenges you will confront building with these materials?

- Do you have any strategies in mind for dealing with those challenges?

After a few minutes, tell them they will have an opportunity to build with one material at a time. Ask them questions, such as the following:

- What might you try to build with these materials?

- Any particular reason you might try that kind of structure?

List responses on the chart, "What I Might Try to Build." Encourage teachers to answer as they feel comfortable—many will not want to commit to a particular kind of structure beforehand, but encourage them to describe the kinds of things they might try.

2. **GIVE INSTRUCTIONS** (5 minutes) for the exploration. Ask teachers to form groups of three or four and to find space on the floor or a table where they can build with one of the materials. Depending on the number of participants and the amounts and variety of materials, they will probably have to share. But keep group size to a minimum to increase engagement. Remind people to try to pay attention to the kinds of interactions you are having with them, as you will be modeling some strategies that can be applied to their own teaching, even though their responses are likely to differ from those of their children.

3. **HELP TEACHERS GET STARTED** (15 minutes). As teachers build with one material at a time, have them try all kinds of structures. Encourage them to talk about what they have found and what they have built. You might want to make a drawing of one or two of their structures. Make comments or ask questions that encourage people to be descriptive, such as the following:

- You seem to be building something long (or tall). Is there any particular reason you chose to do this?

- What characteristics of this material are important for your building (such as size, weight, or shape)?

- Did you have a plan before you built, or are you making decisions as you go along?

4. **CHANGE BUILDING MATERIALS** (20 minutes). Have teachers switch to a different material so that each group will have some open-ended time with two of the materials. Continue to model the teacher's role. Try to get at the science of what they are doing as you interact with them. Ask questions, such as the following:

- Did you have a reason for placing that block there? (Point to a particular section of their building.)

- What would happen if you put another layer on? Or used foam blocks to do that? Or took that block off?

5. **Bring the teachers together for a twenty-minute science talk.** Facilitate a reflective discussion about teachers' building experiences. List their ideas on the chart, "What We Learned about Building Structures." Encourage participants to use their buildings to illustrate and provide evidence for their ideas. Ask probing questions to get the details of what they experienced and the successful strategies they developed. You might ask for a group to tell you about the foundation of their building, why they chose those particular materials and design. This conversation should focus on the design of their structures, the characteristics of the materials they were using, how these helped or hindered their building, and the strategies they used to build stable structures.

During the science talk, help teachers compare what they actually built with what they predicted they would build during your introduction to their building experience. This might uncover additional building challenges they faced.

> **An example of probing questions:**
> "You were building a tower by stacking the foam blocks? . . . How high did you get? . . . And then what happened? . . . Why do you think it fell over? . . . What do others think? . . . What might you do differently next time?"

The Science (55 minutes)

Purpose: Inquiry is a concept that is central to science and should be a part of all science education. Therefore, one of the teacher's primary goals is to help children experience and use the processes of inquiry, integrating them into their daily experiences. It is also key to the teaching approach. The science content is another important feature of *Building Structures with Young Children*. It is central to every building experience and conversation. The inquiry and content are introduced here and will be reinforced throughout the workshops.

1. **Introduce the concept of inquiry** (10 minutes). Tell teachers that they have been engaged in a part of the process of inquiry and that inquiry is a central idea in science and *Building Structures with Young Children*. Refer them to the inquiry diagram on p. 74 of the teacher's guide as you show overhead 1.2: Inquiry diagram. Make the following points as you talk about the diagram.

   - *It is a dynamic process.*
     This process is cyclical in nature. It cannot be fully represented in a linear two-dimensional diagram.

   - *It begins with engagement and wondering.*
     Experience with things, materials, and events is the basis of inquiry. This is a time for play. At this point, the teachers and children are noticing characteristics of building materials and what they will do. You may wonder about many things: how you can build a building like the firehouse down the street, what materials work best for making castles, or how to make a building with space on the inside.

- *Wondering leads to more focused observation and questions.*
  As you explore, you may have lots of questions. I wonder how many I can stack on top of one another before it falls? How can I create a bridge for my cars? Some people ask their questions; others may reveal their questions through actions. Repeated trial and error means you have an idea of what you want your structure to look like and are trying to find a way to do it.

- *Questions focus observation and lead to investigation.*
  In order to pursue something in depth, a single question needs to be identified and refined. There are many kinds of questions. At this point, you and the children need to consider which questions can be answered through simple investigations or which can be modified and pursued through investigation. Ask predicting questions, such as "What will happen if . . ."

- *Investigation is a cyclical process.*
  Investigations begin with a focus or question: What strategies and materials are effective in building tall towers? What are the right materials and shapes for making stable, strong roofs? They involve planning, observing closely, recording experiences, and reflecting in order to identify patterns and construct theories and explanations. New questions arise and are pursued. With your guidance, the children can engage in this experimental stage of inquiry.

- *Share, discuss, reflect, and draw conclusions.*
  This is a time for making meaning of investigations. In small and large groups, you and the children share and form simple ideas and generalizations that will deepen their understanding of the concepts being explored.

2. Reflect on the role inquiry played in their exploration (15 minutes). Ask teachers what aspects of the diagram describe experiences they had during the exploration. Here are some guiding questions:

   - How would you describe the inquiry you just engaged in? Did you experience particular aspects of the diagram during your exploration? What are they?

   - Which questions drove your investigation?

   - What kind of data did you collect related to your questions? How did you document the data?

   Now help them think more analytically about their inquiry:

   - Did identifying questions play a role in your building? What role did it play?

   - How did you use the data you collected? (Ask for specifics and about insights they might have had as they documented.)

   - What evidence influenced you to change your thinking?

   - When and how did you draw some conclusions?

As you make specific connections between their activity and the diagram, emphasize the following:

- Questions and focused activity grow out of an early period of engagement called "open exploration."

- Questions help focus observation and create the need to collect data.

- Sharing ideas exposes one to more data and to different perspectives and ideas, and opens new doors for investigation.

- Recording data as it is collected is useful because it provides a reference for analysis.

- Science is grounded in evidence. Inquiry is about finding the evidence.

3. **INTRODUCE THE SCIENCE CONCEPTS** (25 minutes) by saying that your questions and comments during their exploration were designed to help the teachers focus on particular science concepts. Refer them to descriptions of the science concepts that appear in "Getting Ready" on p. 13 of the teacher's guide. Suggest marking the page with a self-adhesive note for quick reference. Review overhead 1.3.

OVERHEAD 1.3: SCIENCE CONCEPTS

- **Forces: gravity, tension, and compression**
  Gravity is the attraction that bodies exert on one another. The force between the earth and other bodies such as structures is strong because the earth is so big. Structures have to be built so that they resist the pull of gravity and stand up. As children build, they all learn by trial and error to use materials and designs that lead to stability. Try to identify experiences from the teacher's exploration that would be examples of this.

  Some parts of a structure are pressed and squeezed together. That force is called compression. *A tower of blocks is a good example, as the blocks on the bottom of the tower are under compression. Wood can withstand this compression better than certain types of foam.*

  Other parts of a structure are pulled apart. That force is called tension. *Tension is often an issue when working with straws and connectors. Tension pulls them apart at the corners, and the straws often become disconnected from the connectors.*

- **Certain designs are stronger and more stable**
  A structure has to be designed so that it counteracts the force of gravity. It must be built so it is balanced and the forces on it are in equilibrium; otherwise, it will tip or collapse or parts will break. It must be built with a strong enough foundation and a relatively low center of gravity so it doesn't collapse under its own weight or tip easily. Children learn as they build that if the base of a building is narrow and we attempt to build a larger section higher up, their structure will likely fall or be unstable.

- **Different building materials have different characteristics**
  Building materials (such as wood, foam, or plastic) have characteristics that affect building. Some can be pulled hard before they break; some are flexible and bend; others can have a lot of weight put on them without breaking. Things you build with (such as blocks and straws) have different sizes, shapes, and textures. The characteristics of building materials are important to consider when designing and building structures. For example, a tall structure built with foam blocks might not be the best for withstanding wind.

Relate the science concepts to their explorations by reviewing the chart, "What We Learned about Building Structures" and asking them to relate each of the listed learnings to the science concepts. Encourage participants to come up with an example of how they may have been exposed to that concept during their exploration.

4. **CONCLUDE THE WORKSHOP** (5 minutes) by telling teachers that they will have more opportunities to engage in and talk about inquiry, the science concepts, and the teaching approach in future workshops. You might want to collect "Read and Reflect 1" to get a better understanding of what teachers are thinking. Thank teachers for their participation. Give them "Read and Reflect 2," and confirm the time and place for the next workshop.

READ AND REFLECT 1: INTRODUCTION TO *BUILDING STRUCTURES WITH YOUNG CHILDREN*

Name: _____

Before coming to workshop 1, read the introduction to the teacher's guide and the excerpts from a teacher's journal. Respond to these questions as you reflect on what you read. This information will be helpful in the workshop discussion.

1. As you read about teachers A, B, and C, did you make connections to your own teaching? Which teacher was most like you?

2. What were the similarities?

3. What challenges will you face in learning the approach of teacher C?

READ AND REFLECT 2:
GETTING READY

Name: _____

Before coming to workshop 2, read "Getting Ready" as well as the "Books and Web sites" sections in "Resources" at the back of the teacher's guide. Copy and complete the building structures environment checklist in the appendices. Once it is complete, reflect on the following questions. This information will be helpful in the workshop discussion.

1. What are the strengths of your environment? What important elements do you have for your exploration of nature?

2. What challenges do you face? What important elements are you missing?

Getting Ready

AT A GLANCE

Purpose:
- Gain understanding of the important elements of a science-rich learning environment
- Assess needs of own environment and plan for adaptations
- Begin to understand how children's block play is connected to science concepts and inquiry skills

Activity	Time: 1.5 hours	Materials
Overview of Building Environment Discuss important elements of a building environment that encourages an exploration of building structures using photos for analysis.	30 minutes	• Overhead projector, screen, and overheads 2.1–2.4 • Chart: "Creating a Science-Rich Environment"
Preparing Your Own Environment Guide teachers as they assess their own building environments and consider ways to modify their classrooms that will stimulate building.	30 minutes	
Understanding Children's Block Play Use the vignette to illustrate children's block play and the teacher's role.	30 minutes	• Overhead projector, screen, and overheads 2.5 and 2.6 • Copies of the vignette observation form and transcript to video vignette 2, and "Read and Reflect 3" • VCR, monitor, and video cued to vignette 2

Preassignment: Read "Getting Ready" and "Books and Web sites," and complete the "Classroom Environment Checklist" on p. 90 of the teacher's guide. Complete the reflection questions.

Basic Workshop 2: Getting Ready

OBJECTIVES

- Gain understanding of the important elements of a science-rich learning environment
- Assess needs of own environment and plan for adaptations
- Begin to understand how children's block play is connected to science concepts and inquiry skills

OVERVIEW

- Overview of building environment (30 minutes)
- Preparing your own environment (30 minutes)
- Understanding children's block play (30 minutes)

INSTRUCTOR PREPARATION

- **PREVIEW VIGNETTE 2** and identify the points you want to make during the discussion. Refer to the following video instructions.
- **REMIND TEACHERS TO BRING THEIR "CLASSROOM ENVIRONMENT CHECKLIST."**

MATERIALS

- Overhead projector, screen, and overheads 2.1–2.6
- Copies of vignette observation form, the transcript to video vignette 2, and "Read and Reflect 3"
- VCR, monitor, and video cued to vignette 2
- Chart: "Creating a Science-Rich Environment"

Activity

OVERVIEW OF BUILDING ENVIRONMENT (30 MINUTES)

PURPOSE: The environment is key to the children's experience. It should be stimulating and challenging and materials must be accessible. This conversation and photographs will call teachers' attention to important strategies.

1. **INTRODUCE THE TOPIC OF BUILDING ENVIRONMENTS** (10 minutes). Explain the importance of creating an environment that stimulates inquiry about structures and motivates building. Creating this kind of environment means more than providing a block area; it is about selection of building materials, their arrangement, the kind of space available, and the displays and resources that provide ideas about building and structures. Suggest that teachers review the section of the teacher's guide that talks about building environments, and give them a chance to share strategies they are thinking about. List responses on the chart you prepared, "Creating a Science-Rich Environment."

2. Discuss creating an environment that encourages building structures
(20 minutes) using overheads 2.1–2.4.

- If you have time, print the overheads on paper and place each on a piece of newsprint. Mount these around the room and ask teachers in teams to write on each chart how this particular environment encourages inquiry. Bring teachers together and read the responses on the chart. Add important ideas to the chart you have started.

- If you are running behind schedule, use the overheads as overheads and discuss each as you project it, getting ideas about the photo from the teachers and adding important ideas that aren't mentioned.

Overhead 2.1:

How does this environment encourage building structures?

Talk about the large space and how this allows several groups of children enough space to build without interfering with each other. You can also talk about the varied blocks—cardboard bricks, unit blocks, and the foam pieces (on the shelf to the right)—and how they provide an opportunity to explore the characteristics of building materials and how these characteristics affect stability and balance. The displays can also be mentioned—they appear to be documentation panels with pictures of the children at work. You might also mention the importance of a plain surface on the floor. Rugs with bold patterns make it hard for some children to see their buildings.

OVERHEAD 2.2:

How does this environment encourage building structures?

This wall in a block area has posters that are meant to stimulate building. Point out the combination of the photos of a child at work, of a building with windows, and of a brick wall. The city scene with the Conoco sign offers things to talk about, such as how they were able to get that sign to stand up. Note the way the building-related books are displayed.

OVERHEAD 2.3:

How does this environment encourage building structures?

Note the displays again. They combine children's work and a picture of the Eiffel Tower. To the left it looks like a picture of a house with a pitched roof. The child is building with unit blocks, but there are interesting roof pieces and some interesting-looking curved blocks in the background on the right.

OVERHEAD 2.4:

How does this environment encourage building structures?

Note the blocks in the sand table. The sand presents an interesting challenge—creating balance and stability on a soft base. Also note the picture of the house on the wall.

PREPARING YOUR OWN ENVIRONMENT (30 MINUTES)

PURPOSE: An environment that encourages building is carefully thought out and prepared. Assessing the strengths and needs of their own environments is the first step in preparing teachers for a building exploration with children.

1. **IDENTIFY STRENGTHS FROM THE "CLASSROOM ENVIRONMENT CHECKLIST"** (10 minutes). Ask the teachers to get out their classroom environment checklists and their reflections. Ask, "What do you have to help you create a rich environment for young builders?" Connect teachers' resources to the chart of ideas they have made with you. Find out if any of them have things they can share or sources others should know about.

2. **DISCUSS ENVIRONMENT NEEDS** (20 minutes). Discuss one category at a time as you review the needs they have identified and help them think about solutions. The box below has suggestions for addressing each category. Before solving problems, give other teachers a chance to share their strategies, asking, "Does anyone have a suggestion for . . . ?"

Use these questions, based on the checklist, to facilitate the conversation. Focus on helping teachers with their needs.

- Do you all have enough variety and quantity of building materials?

- Did anyone have issues providing space for buildings and displays?

- Did any of you find challenges with your schedule?

- Do you have extra adults to help?

- How are you going to find appropriate children's books?

This is an opportunity to reinforce the value of materials and time in inquiry science. Pursue these issues with a focus on solving them rather than communicating that they are not important.

- **Materials:** A variety of building materials is essential to a successful building exploration. Materials also need to be available in a sufficient quantity for the creation of complex structures by small groups of children who are working collaboratively. Allow the teachers to share what materials they have and what their issues are. If quantity is a problem but they have a variety of materials, they might pool their supplies and rotate them from classroom to classroom. For example, they might put several small sets of Cuisenaire rods together and take turns using them. This would not work for unit blocks, since they should be available in quantity all the time. If having a variety of materials is the problem, think about local businesses that might make a donation or brainstorm with them about how to get recycled materials. If you do discuss recycled materials, review the characteristics of good recycled materials for building:

  - Many pieces in uniform shapes

  - At least some flat sides for building up or creating collage representations

  - Varied sizes, densities, and materials (such as wood, plastic, foam, or cardboard)

  - Different kinds of paper and cardboard for representation work

  You might want to mention that materials such as Legos and Duplos are not appropriate in this exploration. Because they stick together, these materials do not encourage children to explore their own thinking about what makes a strong structure or how materials balance. Suggest that teachers temporarily put them away.

- **Space:** Children must be comfortable as they build structures in the classroom. This might require increasing the size of the block area or adding more building centers (step 4 of "Getting Ready," p. 18 of the teacher's guide, describes these spaces). It is also important to have space at the children's eye level to display children's work and other posters or pictures that will pique interest. Allow teachers to share strategies here—they are often dealing with space constraints and may have developed unique approaches to share. Sometimes it is necessary to rearrange the room for a period of time to accommodate a special focus. The room can always be returned to its original order when the exploration of structures is over.

- **Time:** Children need ample time to experience the world of building structures in a way that builds understanding. Suggest that teachers allow at least thirty to forty-five minutes of focused building time several times a week to get children deeply involved in an exploration and see it through. Help teachers find ways to create blocks of time without unnecessary transitions. Remind them to allow a regular time for science talks.

- **Adults:** Although not absolutely necessary, extra adults are a big help, especially on walks. A letter to families (p. 83 in the teacher's guide) can often generate support and volunteers. Sometimes, however, volunteers are unavailable. Suggest teachers ask their administrator to help find an interested civic group, such as a local literacy organization or Chamber of Commerce.

- **Resources:** Hopefully everyone uses the library. If not, help them locate the nearest branch. You might also have them share ideas for guest experts (such as contractors or architects) who could supply blueprints or designs and even visit their classroom. Briefly mention the importance of additional resources and point out that an annotated list of recommended books is included on p. 82 of the teacher's guide, as well as suggestions for guest experts on p. 69.

Understanding Children's Block Play (30 minutes)

Purpose: This activity will help teachers begin to observe their children's block play, think about who is building, find ways to encourage those who aren't building, and observe the block play themes. At the same time they will begin to understand the teacher's role in connecting science learning to children's ongoing dramatic and constructive play.

1. **Provide an overview of the nature of children's block play** (10 minutes). Introduce the discussion by sharing the ideas on overheads 2.5 and 2.6. Ask for examples of children's recent block play from their classrooms as you make the following connections.

Overhead 2.5: Types of Block Play

- **Constructive**
  Constructive play permeates what children build. Whenever they are engaged in manipulating objects to create a construction, they are engaged in constructive play. We encourage this type of play by providing enough space and varied materials for building.

- **Dramatic and symbolic play**
  Block play is often motivated by an interest in dramatic play. An interest in stories with police stations, farms, or castles leads to building these structures. You can build on these interests by providing props that will entice builders into the block area and by encouraging children to assume the role of a construction worker or an architect. Much of block play is symbolic, that is, the children use the building materials to symbolize something else (such as bricks, an elevator, or a car) or create a structure that is a symbol (such as a letter, face, or police station).

- **Exploratory**
  Exploratory play describes the children's interest in the actual building process. As children work to find effective strategies for achieving balance, stability, and strength in their buildings, they are engaged in exploratory play.

Use overhead 2.6 to discuss some of the influences on children's play.

Overhead 2.6: Influences on Block Play

- **Previous experience**
  The ideas and abilities children bring to teachers' classroom block areas have in part grown from previous building experiences. While some children may have had no previous experience, others may have construction toys at home or a family member who gave them scraps of wood or other materials to build with. Experience might also determine their interests. While children in New York might gravitate to building skyscrapers, children in Iowa might initially be more interested in farms. Use of books and posters can broaden children's knowledge about the types of buildings they could build.

- **Culture**
  Culture also influences children's building. Girls from some cultures might think that building is for boys. It will be important to find ways of interesting them. Table blocks, creating a "Girls' Day" in the block area, and building houses or furniture for stuffed animals or dolls can all be effective strategies.

- **Development**
  Children's cognitive, social, and physical development all influence their capacity to build. Frequent experiences with blocks, support for their problem solving, and encouragement of collaboration will all strengthen their development in important ways.

---

2. INTRODUCE VIGNETTE 2 (20 MINUTES). Explain that this vignette, which was filmed in a Boston kindergarten, shows a variety of block play. It provides ways a teacher can encourage constructive, dramatic, and exploratory play while making important connections to science learning.

   a. Distribute the transcript and the vignette observation form, and tell teachers they will use this form to take notes as they view the video, noting children's engagement and the strategies the teacher uses to encourage engagement and inquiry.

   b. Show the vignette.

   c. After the viewing, discuss observations connecting what teachers have seen to overhead 2.5: Types of Block Play. Ask the following questions:

   - What types of block play did you see in this vignette?

   - In what ways did the teacher encourage these types of play?

   - How did she connect the play to science learning?

Look for responses like these:

- Types of play—All block play is constructive. The girls shown in the vignette are busy constructing a variety of structures. In the beginning, there is a hint at their exploratory play when the child is working to balance the blocks at the top of her building. The child describing how her building looks like a person is a beautiful example of symbolic play. The fact that they are all building houses for the teacher and her parents suggests dramatic play, as does the sequence in which they are talking about where the children will be.

- Teacher encouragement—The teacher is encouraging her children in a number of ways. First, she is seated on the floor with them at children's level, which is a powerful form of encouragement. Second, she shows interest in their buildings in various ways, including questioning what they are building, her invitation to a party, and her comparison of two houses that are wider and skinnier.

- Connection to science learning—The teacher makes important connections to the science. By talking about hurricanes, strong houses, and good strong roofs, she is calling attention to design features and encouraging the children to think about strength in their building.

---

3. CONCLUDE THE WORKSHOP by telling teachers the concrete ways you will support them as they set up their environments. You might want to collect "Read and Reflect 2" in order to better understand their environment issues. Distribute "Read and Reflect 3," review your expectations, and confirm the time and place for the next workshop.

BASIC WORKSHOP 2: VIGNETTE OBSERVATION FORM

Name: _____

Note your observations by identifying the teacher strategies and child responses.

- Types of play the children are engaged in (such as constructive, dramatic, symbolic, exploratory)
- Ways the teacher encourages building
- Ways the teacher makes connections to science concepts

Teacher Strategy	Child Response

TRANSCRIPT OF VIDEO VIGNETTE 2: HAWAIIAN HOUSES

Scene: Four girls along with their teacher are building with unit blocks. The setting is the block area of a Boston kindergarten.

The children: Jamaya, Clarissa, Hannah, and Megan

Teacher: Do you know which one is the mistake? Lavino can show you. Lavino, can you show her the mistake?

Child: Oh, oh.

Teacher: Okay, where's Clarissa?

Megan: Where's the *(inaudible)*?

Megan: I'm weighing out some bricks.

Jamaya: It looks like the person.

Teacher: It does look like a person. What part is this part of the person? *(Teacher points to structure.)*

Jamaya: Head.

Teacher: And then [what] part is this?

Jamaya: T-shirt.

Teacher: The T-shirt. And then what part is this?

Jamaya: The pants.

Teacher: Oh, yeah, it looks a lot like a person.

Jamaya: Make sure you don't mess up my *(inaudible)*.

Teacher: I promise I will not touch your structure. Wow, you can see all the way down to the bottom. You can see the carpet in there.

Child: Oh, yeah. Cool.

Teacher: So what is this structure for? What does it do?

Jamaya: It's . . . it's something from . . . it's something for *(inaudible)*.

Teacher: Okay, you're not going to tell me until later?

Jamaya: When I'm done.

Teacher: Okay, when you're done.

Jamaya: Tell who it is.

Teacher: Okay. Clarissa, will you tell me about your structure?

Clarissa: It's a big house.

Teacher: That's a really long house, huh?

Teacher: I will in a minute, *(inaudible)*. So what's this big part?

Clarissa: It's a *(inaudible)*.

Teacher: And I noticed that you put some blocks to keep the water in. That was a good idea—so the water doesn't go in the house.

Hannah: It's a *(inaudible)* really, really small *(inaudible)*.

Megan: Or we could do that. And you have kids and they will be scared to go out that side.

Teacher: Oops, I'm sorry. I know I had *(inaudible)* on today.

Megan: Look through there. *(Megan looks through structure.)*

Teacher: Excellent. You're all done? Oh, now you're going to tell me who lives in it? Who lives in it?

Jamaya: Miss Bond.

Teacher: I live in it? That's great. Show me my house. You know what I noticed, Jamaya? My house is about the same size as my mom and dad's house. But my mom and dad's house is wider and my house is skinnier.

Jamaya: I want to make it tall like the other way.

Child: This is your house.

Teacher: This one's my house too?

Child: Yeah, but . . .

Teacher: I have a lot of houses.

Hannah: Don't look at it.

Child: And I'm making a house for you right here.

Teacher: Okay, I'm not looking.

Child: . . . for you right here too.

Teacher: Oh, my goodness.

Child: Miss Bond, I'm going to put some more *(inaudible)*.

Teacher: When you're all done, when you're done building my houses, can I invite you over for a party?

All: Yes.

Child: Miss Bond.

Teacher: I'll be there in just a moment. Tell me when you're done with this story, okay? Tell me when you're done with the story.

Hannah: I can't look.

Teacher: It's wiggling a little, huh? Are these houses in Hawaii?

All: Yes.

Teacher: Oh, they are . . . oh, okay. You know what? In Hawaii sometimes they have things like hurricanes that have really strong, strong, strong winds, almost like tornado strong. And so I hope that you build the house really strong so that when I'm in it and there's a hurricane, that nothing will happen to the house. Make sure it's really, really strong.

Child: Yeah, *(inaudible)*.

Teacher: So nothing happens to the house?

Child: No.

Teacher: You're going to make it . . . oh, you're going to make sure that it's "volcano proof" too. To make sure that a volcano with the lava . . .

Hannah: No, no, it's made out of cement.

Teacher: Oh. Made out of cement—that's a good idea.

Hannah: Our house is made out of cement.

Clarissa: *(Blows on house with teacher.)*

Teacher: Oh, yeah, so that's lucky, if I was . . . if there was a hurricane, where do you think . . . like where's . . . Okay, if this is me right here, where do you think I should stay if there's a hurricane, where in your house? Can you show me where you think I should stay? Where would be a good place for me to stay if there was a hurricane?

Clarissa: Right [here]. *(Clarissa points and knocks down some blocks.)*

Teacher: Why?

Clarissa: Because . . . because that . . . that will keep you from hurricane.

Teacher: That will keep me from the hurricane? I think that's a good idea.

Clarissa: And that will keep you not cold.

Teacher: Oh, that's a good idea too. And it's really . . . this is a good strong roof right here and I don't think the wind will blow on me either—right? And the rain—there's a lot of rain in hurricanes too. And if you were in Hawaii with me too, then I would invite you to my strong house, too, so that you could be safe too.

READ AND REFLECT 3:
OPEN EXPLORATION

Name: _____

Read and Reflect

Before coming to workshop 3, read the open exploration and science teaching sections in the teacher's guide. Respond to these questions as you reflect on what you read. This information will be helpful in the workshop discussion.

We will talk about the following two purposes of open exploration. What examples of these can you find in the open exploration steps? Be specific and note the page numbers of your reference.

1. Gives the children opportunities to wonder, notice, and explore. How exactly does open exploration do this?

2. Gives the children the support, materials, and time they need to begin their exploration. When and how does open exploration do this?

You should also answer these questions:
- How do you see involving families in these explorations? What will the benefit be to you and to the children?
- What challenges will you face as you implement open exploration for the first time?

Observe and Record
- Observe children's block building over the course of one week and record what you see. Look for the kinds of play children are engaged in (such as constructive, dramatic, or exploratory), who is playing, and the interests being expressed. Bring this information to workshop 3.

Overview of Open Exploration

AT A GLANCE

Purpose:
- Become familiar with open exploration, its purpose, and the cycle of activity
- Gain basic understanding of the teacher's role during open exploration
- Begin to understand how children might engage in open exploration

Activity	Time	Materials
Overview of Open Exploration Introduce the purpose and flow of open exploration and help teachers connect this information to their exploration from workshop 1.	45 minutes	• Overhead projector, screen, and overheads 3.1 and 3.2
Examine Young Children's Open Exploration Support teachers as they discuss their assessment of block play. Use the vignette to illustrate open exploration and its connection with children's building experiences.	45 minutes	• VCR, monitor, and video cued to vignette 3 • Copies of the vignette observation form and transcript to video vignette 3, and "Read and Reflect 4"

Preassignment: Read "Open Exploration," "Observation and Assessment," and "Involving Families" in the teacher's guide and complete reflection questions.
- Observe children's block building, referring to "Read and Reflect 3" for guidance.

Basic Workshop 3: Overview of Open Exploration

OBJECTIVES

- Become familiar with open exploration, its purpose, and the cycle of activity
- Gain basic understanding of the teacher's role during open exploration
- Begin to understand how children might engage in open exploration

OVERVIEW

- Overview of open exploration (45 minutes)
- Examine young children's open exploration (45 minutes)

INSTRUCTOR PREPARATION

- **PREVIEW VIGNETTE 3** and identify the points you want to make during the discussion. Refer to the following video instructions.

MATERIALS

- Overhead projector, screen, and overheads 3.1 and 3.2
- VCR, monitor, and video cued to vignette 3
- Copies of vignette observation form, the transcript to video vignette 3, and "Read and Reflect 4"

Activity

OVERVIEW OF OPEN EXPLORATION (45 MINUTES)

PURPOSE: As teachers prepare to use open exploration, they will need to think about three aspects of the curriculum:

- The sequence of steps and types of experiences children will have
- The role of the teacher as a facilitator of science inquiry
- Young children's early engagement with building structures

1. **PROVIDE AN OVERVIEW OF OPEN EXPLORATION** (30 minutes) using overheads 3.1 and 3.2.

   a. Discuss the purpose of open exploration using overhead 3.1. Mention that teachers have engaged in an open exploration in workshop 1, making some connection to their experience as you talk.

OVERHEAD 3.1: PURPOSE OF OPEN EXPLORATION

- **Give children opportunities to wonder, notice, and explore.**
  Wonder, noticing, and exploring mark children's entry into inquiry. A carefully planned environment and teacher support are keys to open exploration. Use individual children's interests as a starting point for their engagement in dramatic or constructive play and thus in the building structures exploration. Early theories about balance and stability, as well as different materials and designs, can be drawn out as children talk about their building experiences.

- **Give children the support, materials, and time they need to begin their exploration.**
  Time and a variety of materials are essential to open exploration for building the base of experience that prepares children for their later focused investigations. In these early building experiences, children learn about the characteristics of the materials and what can be done with them. Teachers notice children's interests, questions, and the challenges they face as they struggle with construction problems. This information is used to encourage engagement and focus experiences.

Ask teachers for examples of these purposes from the teacher's guide, as per the reading assignment. You might also ask what they noticed about the instructions and which features they will find especially helpful as they use the teacher's guide. Ask teachers to be specific, citing page numbers for easy reference.

This conversation is designed to help teachers learn to navigate the teacher's guide. The ideas of those who have taken a careful look will help those who are feeling overwhelmed. Look for answers such as these:

Introduce the children to building materials:

- In step 1 the children share previous experiences and describe things they have done with blocks.
- In step 2 the children are introduced to new materials, reluctant builders are encouraged, and they begin walkabouts and science talks—where they talk about the ways they are using the blocks.

Introduce the children to appropriate ways of using various building centers:

- In step 1 they plan rules for builders and revisit these rules after they have been used for a while.
- Rules are reinforced through conversations about the children's productive building experiences.

Children begin to engage in inquiry:

- The teacher models wonder and questioning in conversations.
- The teacher models recording, representing, and using descriptive language when talking about buildings.
- In step 2 the teacher introduces new materials, and challenges are offered to stimulate investigations.
- A walkabout encourages the children to notice each other's work and discussions of building issues and strategies in step 2. A vocabulary for building is established for use in reflective conversations.
- Science talks encourage reflection in step 2.

b. Present the flow of open exploration using overhead 3.2.

OVERHEAD 3.2: FLOW OF OPEN EXPLORATION

- **Step 1: Introduce children to building structures**
This step has three key parts:

  1. *Talk about prior building experiences and introduce the building materials children will be using. This introduction sets the stage by saying this activity is important, you as a teacher value it, and there are particular ways to engage in it.*

  2. *Choice time provides the essential early experiences that will continue throughout the exploration.*

  3. *Sharing children's previous building experiences contributes to the classroom culture of inquiry, helping children learn to talk about their buildings and their ideas about building, and is key to children's science learning.*

- **Step 2: Ongoing exploration and reflections**
Introduce new materials and props, acknowledge block play, encourage reluctant builders to share and reflect using walkabouts, and continue science talks.

Make these points as you talk about open exploration:

- The guide provides detailed instructions that teachers can follow for each step.

- All children will need a period of open exploration to become familiar with the materials and how to use them effectively.

- Open exploration will vary depending on children's prior experience and their developmental levels. Have they built with materials in preschool or at home? If so, they will need less time in open exploration—some children may take a week or two; others may take most of the exploration.

    c. Emphasize the importance of sending home the family letter in the involving families section of the teacher's guide. Also, mention the assessment and observation section. Note the value of copying the observation record and using it regularly during the exploration.

2. **DISCUSS THEIR OBSERVATIONS** (15 minutes) about the types of block play and the influences on children's block play. Reinforce points made earlier during workshop 2. Ask the following questions:

   - *What kinds of block play did you see in your classrooms?*
   Encourage them to use the words *constructive, dramatic,* and *exploratory* and to give specific examples. Probe until you get enough information to understand the connections they are making.

   - *Who is playing with blocks and who is not?*
   Be sure that teachers understand that one of their goals is to encourage everyone's engagement. Identify problems and help them find solutions.

   - *What interests are being expressed?*
   Help teachers figure out that the kinds of building are the starting points for encouraging further inquiry. This early observation and sharing will set the stage for future conversations about their progress.

EXAMINE YOUNG CHILDREN'S OPEN EXPLORATION (45 MINUTES)

PURPOSE: The analysis of a video vignette will give teachers a chance to see children engaged in open exploration. Readings from the teacher's guide, teachers' own exploration, and your presentation about open exploration will take on new meaning when teachers observe children's interactions with materials and each other.

1. **DISCUSS CHILDREN'S EARLY BUILDING EXPERIENCES** (10 minutes). Mention that most children have a natural desire to build and will construct with anything they can find. You may have an example to share or want teachers to share observations they have about this idea. Go on to explain that it is only through many and varied experiences that children develop from the early stages of block building to being more capable builders who can reflect on their building.

   Ask for observations of early building experiences, being sure that the following approaches are mentioned:

   - Taking the blocks off the shelf but not doing much with them
   - Covering the floor space by building horizontally
   - Stacking and loving to watch the blocks fall

   Add that over time, children become better able to build structures with some stability. Through trial and error, they learn to place blocks carefully on top of each other. They will also learn what materials, sizes, and shapes work best for different purposes.

2. **SHOW VIGNETTE 3** (15 minutes). Explain that this vignette was filmed in the block area of a Boston Head Start. There are five children building and four of them are English language learners. Share that the teachers' interactions are designed to support the language learning of these children. If the teachers in your group have English language learners, you may want the teachers to pay attention to that element of the vignette. Mention that you will show the vignette twice. In the first viewing, ask the teachers to focus on the types of play they are seeing and children's abilities and interests.

   a. Distribute the transcript and the vignette observation form.

   b. Show the vignette.

   c. After the viewing, discuss observations of the children's building experiences. Try to steer away from discussing the teacher, saving those comments for the second viewing. Ask the following questions:

      - What types of play did you see?
      - What did you notice about the children's abilities and interests?

Look for responses like these:

- Types of play—The children are clearly engaged in constructive play. That they have houses in mind and are using blocks to represent people suggests some dramatic play. Their efforts to build tall implies that they are engaged in exploratory play, looking for effective strategies to achieve balance and stability as they build taller and taller.

- Abilities and interests—These children are interested in building and their motivation lies in the exploratory aspect of what they are doing. They have some understanding of how to use the materials in order to create structures of this kind, which suggests that they are not beginning builders. While Victor does not know the protocol for placing blocks on someone else's building, you see some nice collaboration between Armin and James as they figure out how to place a block on the top of their tower.

- Experiences with science concepts—These children are exploring the challenge of creating tall buildings that are strong and stable or balanced. They are learning what blocks to use, how to place them on top of each other, and what kind of foundation they need. Although we have not seen experimentation with different kinds of blocks, they may have had experiences with foam or some material other than wood and found it was not as effective.

3. **SHOW THE VIGNETTE AGAIN** (15 minutes). A second viewing of vignette 3 will allow teachers to focus more on their role. Remind them to take notes in the second column of the observation form. After the viewing, ask what they noticed about the teacher and the role she played.

Make these points about the teacher's approach to teaching and learning:

- Reinforces rules or procedures for building when she talks about the need for space, puts some of the blocks away, and allows paths for walking without disturbing certain buildings.

- Shares her own observations in a way that calls attention to the strategies being used by describing Thalia's building: how straight it is, the use of rectangle blocks, and that it has no brace at the bottom. The comments about James's two towers becoming one does this also.

- Asks the children to compare the height of two towers, which encourages careful noticing and suggests measurement as a part of data collection. They will do more with this later.

- Models methods of recording by getting the camera and mentioning drawing a picture.

- Uses vocabulary words such as *balancing, floor, roof,* and *chimney,* which helps the children build a vocabulary for talking about their buildings, particularly the second language learners. She also uses hand motions to do this.

- Asks Roney about what is going to hold up his roof, challenging him to take on a more complex building question—how to make walls.

4. **CONCLUDE THE WORKSHOP** (5 minutes) by collecting "Read and Reflect 3." Give them "Read and Reflect 4," review your expectations, and confirm the time and place for the next workshop.

Basic Workshop 3: Vignette Observation Form

Name: _____

Viewing 1	Viewing 2
Observe:	Observe:
• Types of play	• Teacher strategies
• Abilities and interests	
• Experiences with science concepts	

Transcript of Video Vignette 3: Open Exploration with Unit Blocks

Scene: Five children—James, Victor, Roney, Armin, and Thalia—are building structures at a Boston Head Start.

Teacher: I see part of your problem. You don't have enough space. You don't have enough space here. You need to put some of these blocks away so you'll have some more space. You can't build without space to build. Okay, look. Roney, is that better?

Roney: Yes.

Teacher: Okay, now you have some space here. Now you can start to build.

Victor: Do you want to make a boat?

Teacher: Wow, whose is this? It's balancing.

Child: It's Ali's.

Teacher: That's Ali's?

Child: Even (inaudible) know how to (inaudible).

Teacher: And he didn't put any here today like he did Monday. He didn't put any underneath like you did on Monday.

Armin: Isn't it like this.

Teacher: Are you making a floor in your house now?

Roney: Yes.

Teacher: Is this the floor in your house?

Roney: No, roof.

Teacher: You're making a roof?

Roney: Roofs.

Teacher: You're making a big roof?

Roney: Yeah.

Teacher: Roney, if you made the floor, now you're going to make the roof?

Roney: Yeah. Up in the sky.

Teacher: What—up in the sky? What's going to hold the roof? What's going to make it stay up?

Roney: I want to hold it.

Teacher: You're going to hold it?

Roney: Yeah.

Teacher: Oh, okay. (To Thalia) Wow, you're balancing. You used the rectangle blocks, didn't you. And you put them very, very straight right on top of each other.

Victor: Be like this. Do something like this.

Teacher: Victor. You know what? Can I hand them to you, because Thalia's working very hard here? What do you want, Victor? Tell me the shape.

Victor: Like this.

(Victor starts to put triangle block on top of Thalia's structure.)

Teacher: Oh, you have to ask Thalia first.

Victor: How I got this one.

Teacher: You have to ask Thalia if it's okay to put it on her building.

Roney: Yeah, I know that.

Teacher: What do you need now, James? I'll pass whatever you need because . . .

James: I need five of those.

Teacher: This kind again? I don't know if I have five.

Victor: This some and this.

Teacher: Okay.

James: Me and (inaudible).

Teacher: James and Victor are using the cylinder blocks—the big cylinders. And Thalia's using the rectangle blocks.

Victor: Yeah. We said (inaudible).

Teacher: And they're getting very tall.

Victor: Yeah, very tall.

James: And this is bigger than Thalia's.

Teacher: Do you think yours is taller than Thalia's? Step back.

James: Yeah, if we put one of those shorter ones.

Teacher: You want this long one? You want to try it?

James: So it can be longer than Thalia's. *(Puts large cylinder block on top of his structure.)*

James: Oh, yeah.

Teacher: Is it taller than Thalia's now?

Victor: Yes. How about we put this there.

Teacher: I think it's a little taller. James, I was wondering . . .

Armin: I want to put this here but just don't lay here.

Teacher: Put that so it doesn't—so the floor doesn't break?

Armin: No, put this.

Teacher: Please be careful when you're walking around Thalia's tower. We wouldn't want to break it. Let me get my camera.

Child: It's a house.

Teacher: It's a house. And are those the people that live in the house?

TRANSCRIPT OF VIDEO VIGNETTE 3: OPEN EXPLORATION WITH UNIT BLOCKS (CONT'D)

James: Yes.

Child: Oh, I'm looking some—

Teacher: And those are the people that live in the house. James, can we make a deal that we'll only walk this way? I'm afraid Thalia's building is going to get bumped.

Roney: Hey. *(Inaudible.)*

Teacher: Tell me about why James—you know—what I noticed about yours?

Armin: Doesn't have to go.

Teacher: That's a tough one, James.

Child: Because it's nice.

Teacher: Are you looking for a triangle block?

Victor: Five of them.

Teacher: Five little . . . What are they, Victor—that you made five of?

Child: I don't *(inaudible)*.

Teacher: Chimneys . . .Are they chimneys in your house, where the smoke comes out?

Victor: No.

Teacher: No.

Victor: On the roof.

Teacher: Part of the roof?

Victor: Yeah, that's what they is.

Teacher: Do you know what I noticed that James did on yours? He made two towers—oops—he made two towers going up. And then he turned it into one tower. James, you know what I noticed about yours? You made two towers going up.

Child: Can I clean that up?

Teacher: And then he made it into one tower. Do you think that makes it stronger?

Victor: *(Nods.)*

Teacher: You think it does? Why do you think it makes it stronger?

READ AND REFLECT 4:
OPEN EXPLORATION

Name: _____

Make a copy of the "Observation Record" on p. 93 of *Building Structures with Young Children*. Document observations of four or five children during an open exploration in the block area. Reflect on your observations and complete the questions below. Bring your observation record and your reflections to workshop 4.

1. What evidence do you see of children's interest in building structures? Include specific comments and behaviors of the children.

2. What connections can you make between children's engagement and the science outcomes on pp. 97–103 of the teacher's guide? Look in the builder behaviors column for examples similar to those of the children.

3. How will you encourage children's open exploration? What might improve the quality of their engagement? How can you extend experiences they have had? How can you draw in new children?

4. How would you rate the quality of your observation notes? Did you record descriptive details that were useful when reflecting? What might you want to do differently next time?

Focused Exploration of Towers

AT A GLANCE

Purpose:
- Engage in a focused exploration of building towers
- Deepen understanding of the science concepts and inquiry skills
- Experience the teacher's role as a facilitator of focused exploration

Activity	Time	Materials
Discuss Observation Ask teachers to share open exploration observations briefly.	20 minutes	
Focused Exploration of Building Towers Facilitate an exploration of building towers with an emphasis on building strategies that provide height and stability. The teachers' role will be modeled by encouraging inquiry and engagement with the science concepts.	1 hour and 10 minutes	• Building materials • Reference books • Charts: "Strategies for Building Strong Towers," "Tower Height," and "Strategies for Focusing Children" • Paper, pencils, and markers • Camera and film (optional) • Copies of "Read and Reflect 5"

Preassignment: Conduct observation of a block play and complete reflection questions.

Basic Workshop 4: Focused Exploration of Towers

OBJECTIVES

- Engage in a focused exploration of building towers
- Deepen understanding of the science concepts and inquiry skills
- Experience the teacher's role as a facilitator of focused exploration

OVERVIEW

- Discuss observation (20 minutes)
- Focused exploration of building towers (1 hour 10 minutes)

INSTRUCTOR PREPARATION

- **REVIEW "FOCUSED EXPLORATION: TOWERS"** in the teacher's guide. You will be modeling an exploration with elements of these steps. This review will help you understand the elements of the exploration and strategies you might use for engaging teachers.
- **SET UP A BUILDING ENVIRONMENT WITH TOWER MATERIALS.** If you are going to have participants work on tables, use small blocks such as Kapla or mini unit blocks. Be sure there are enough for each group of three or four to build tall. Ideally you will have floor space for unit blocks as well. You might want books with pictures.

MATERIALS

- Building materials (provide enough and a variety of different materials for building)
- Reference books (use during the exploration)
- Charts: "Strategies for Building Strong Towers" (make two columns: "Strategy" and "Reason"); "Tower Height" (make two columns: "Tower 1" and "Tower 2"); and "Strategies for Focusing Children"
- Paper, pencils, and markers (use for drawing towers)
- Camera and film (optional)
- Copies of "Read and Reflect 5"

Activity

DISCUSS OBSERVATION (20 MINUTES)

PURPOSE: This brief conversation will give teachers a chance to share experiences and give you some information about their engagement with the material you have presented. Hopefully, they will continue the conversation in informal settings.

Facilitate a brief conversation in which teachers have a chance to share their early experiences with open exploration. You might ask questions like these:

- *What kinds of building are the children doing?*
  Encourage sharing of types of play, developmental information, and interests that are emerging.

- *How are the children showing their interest?*
  They might talk about children's repeated use of the block areas, duration of play, and questions asked or comments made. Be sure this includes mention of who is interested and any issues they are having getting all the children engaged.

- *What connections have you made to the science outcomes?*
  Have them refer to the outcomes listed in the appendix of the teachers' guide so they become used to using this language to describe what they are seeing and the connections they are making to science content and inquiry.

- *What next steps are you planning?*
  Encourage them to refer to the steps in the teacher's guide for ideas, identifying where they are currently and what the guide suggests for next steps.

If issues arise and there is no time to problem solve, be sure to let the teachers know how you will follow up with them.

FOCUSED EXPLORATION OF BUILDING TOWERS (1 HOUR 10 MINUTES)

PURPOSE: This experience will provide teachers with a deeper understanding of focused exploration—its purpose, the nature of activities, and the role that teachers play in facilitating children's inquiry—as well as of the science concepts and the nature of the building materials.

1. **INTRODUCE THE ACTIVITY** (5 minutes). Tell teachers they will be engaged in a focused exploration of towers. Mention that you will be modeling the strategies they can use to engage their children in exploration and inquiry. As with the exploration they did in workshop 1, this exploration has been designed for adults. However, much of this can be used with children.

2. **BEGIN THE EXPLORATION** (10 minutes). Provide the challenge of building towers by first introducing the available materials. Have teachers work in groups of three or four (depending on how much material you have) and quickly build a tower, replicating one they think their children might build.

> During this first exploration, avoid focusing teachers on the forces or the strength and stability of their towers. These concepts and characteristics will be discussed later in the exploration.

As you work with each group, try modeling the teacher's role in the following ways:

- Restate the challenge ("Remember that you are to build as tall as you can.")

- Give positive encouragement ("Wow! You are getting really high.")

- Ask them about the materials they are using ("Why are you putting the colored cubes in the middle?" "You haven't used any of the foam. Why not?")

- Articulate what you see them doing ("I noticed you put all of the blocks on their sides. Is there a reason you don't put them on their ends? What would be different about that?")

3. **DISCUSS THE EXPLORATION** (20 minutes). Give them a minute to first walk around the room and look at the different towers, and then bring teachers together to talk about their exploration of towers and initiate some analysis of what they have done.

   a. Use the following sequence of topics for the discussion:

   - Encourage teachers to make predictions, helping them focus on the structure itself and the science ideas that inform their decisions by asking, "If a big wind were to come through this room, which tower do you think would fall down first? Why do you think so?" "Which tower will be the next to fall? The last? Why do you think so?" This use of inquiry skills—predicting and constructing reasonable explanations—allows teachers to think about the science concepts and what they understand about them, and apply what they know to a concrete task.

   - Ask "what if . . ." questions. ("What do you think would happen if I took this block out?" "What do you think would happen if these were replaced with bigger blocks?")

   - Have them articulate and compare their theories as they make their predictions. ("That is different from Joan's idea. Why do you think yours is likely to be more successful?") This kind of questioning continues their thinking and reflection by challenging them to further refine their explanations with a focus on the science concepts.

   b. Following the discussion, record teachers' ideas about what makes the towers stable and strong on a chart labeled "Strategies for Building Strong Towers" with two columns: "Strategy" and "Reason."

   As you record responses, be sure specific references are made to characteristics of the actual buildings. To encourage their thinking, ask questions such as the following: "Which part is the weakest? How will you know when a section is about to fall? What will happen first?"

   c. Allow a few minutes for teachers to measure the towers, using a tape measure or cutting yarn or string the height of each tower. Create a chart labeled "Tower Height" with two columns: "Tower 1" and "Tower 2." Record tower measurements in the first column.

4. **CONTINUE THE EXPLORATION** (15 minutes). Present teachers with the challenge of building new towers that are taller and stronger. Have them use strategies from their Tower 1 experience and any others they may have discovered. Do the following as you go to each group:

- Observe and listen. Note what teachers are saying and doing, the language they use, their use of strategies from the "Strategies for Building Strong Towers" chart, the level of collaboration among teachers. You can reflect on these things later as you make points about their inquiry.

- Remind teachers of the science. ("Where do you think the weakest point of your structure is? Why do you think that it's weak there? Is it unbalanced? Is it too top-heavy?" "As you work, think about the connection between how the building is designed and how well it stands up.")

- Offer encouragement. ("That looks like a really strong foundation.")

- Restate the challenge. ("Remember, this is about how you can make a tower both taller and stronger.")

- Articulate what you see them doing. ("I noticed you put all the blocks on their side. Is there a reason you don't put them on their ends? What would be different about doing it that way? Why do you think it would be less (or more) strong, taller or less tall?")

- Revisit the list of their strategies. ("Which strategies from our list have you used? How have you used them? Do you think they helped strengthen the building?" "I noticed you are . . . Is that related to one of the strategies on the list or is it something new you are trying? Why are you doing that?") These kinds of questions will help them think about their use of design and materials to create stability.

- Ask about the materials they are using. ("You have chosen to add some foam here. Why?" "Why have you chosen these materials? In what way are they contributing to your tower's height?") Questions like these will help them think about the relationship between the characteristics of the materials as well as stability, height, and strength.

- Encourage them to draw their towers if they finish in time.

- Take photos (optional). Your photos could be used to model documentation panel making for advanced workshop 14.

5. **PROCESS AGAIN** (10 minutes). Have teachers walk around the building environment and look at the new towers. Follow these steps to begin a discussion of strategies for building stronger towers:

   a. Start by taking measurements and writing them in column 2 of the "Tower Height" chart. Note that collecting and recording data is an important inquiry skill. Compare the two lists, noting where the towers are taller and where they are not.

   b. Encourage discussion by asking questions that help teachers look more closely at the process. Starting first with teachers whose towers are taller, ask: "What did you do to get taller this time?"

c. As new strategies come up, write them on the "Tower Height" chart. You might want to place check marks next to strategies listed that were already used.

- Ask more probing questions, getting them to talk about additional building characteristics. Ask questions like these: "Where might there be compression, tension, or instability in your buildings?" "Are certain ways of positioning the materials better than others?" "Are some of the blocks easier to build high with? Why?" "What kinds of design elements help you build high? Why do you think they help?"

6. **TALK ABOUT YOUR ROLE IN THE PREVIOUS EXPLORATION** (10 minutes). Ask, "Was there anything I said or did during this exploration that helped or didn't help you to get involved and engage in inquiry?" Use this conversation as a way to elevate the modeling you have done and call attention to the impact of particular strategies, such as the kinds of questions you asked and the way the activities were structured. Write their responses on the "Strategies for Focusing Children" chart.

> You are looking for teachers to identify the ways in which you have focused them on the science of building—forces, stability and balance, characteristics of materials, elements of design, and so on. You challenged them to engage with the materials and then to think analytically about what they had done. Be sure they identify some specific strategies such as engaging in predicting, guiding them to think about science concepts, collecting and recording relevant data, and helping analyze data.

7. **CONCLUDE THE WORKSHOP** by collecting "Read and Reflect 4." Give them "Read and Reflect 5," review your expectations, and confirm the time and place for the next workshop.

READ AND REFLECT 5:
FOCUSED EXPLORATION

Name: _____

Before coming to workshop 5 read focused exploration and extensions in the teacher's guide. Observe a small group of children (two to four) engaged in building structures and complete an observation record (p. 93 in the teacher's guide). Respond to these questions as you reflect on what you read and observe. This information will be helpful in the workshop discussion. In workshop 5 we will talk about three purposes of focused exploration. What examples of these can you find in the focused exploration steps?

1. Help children gain deeper understandings of building structures. How exactly does focused exploration do this? What teaching strategies (refer to the teacher's role in "Resources") are key?

2. Encourage continued use of the building environment. When and how does focused exploration do this?

3. What challenges will you face as you implement focused exploration for the first time?

Overview of Focused Exploration

AT A GLANCE

Purpose:

- Become familiar with focused exploration, its purpose and its sequence
- Gain basic understanding of the teacher's role during focused exploration
- Continue to build understanding of the science concepts and inquiry skills and how they are expressed in children's behaviors and conversation
- Begin to understand what children's exploration in focused exploration might look like
- Build deeper understanding of the difference between open exploration and focused exploration, as well as the transition between the two

Activity	Time	Materials
Discuss Observations Facilitate a conversation in which teachers share their classroom experiences.	30 minutes	• "Read and Reflect 5" • Overhead projector, screen, and overheads 5.1–5.3 • Chart: "The Teacher's Role"
A Closer Look at Focused Exploration Give teachers an overview of focused exploration, its purpose and flow. Connect their towers exploration to this content. Use a vignette to illustrate what focused exploration looks like in a classroom.	1 hour	• VCR, monitor, and video cued to vignette 4 • Copies of vignette observation form and transcript to video vignette 4, and "Read and Reflect 6"

Preassignment: Read "Focused Exploration" and "Extensions." Conduct an observation and respond to reflection questions.

Basic Workshop 5: Overview of Focused Exploration

OBJECTIVES

- Become familiar with focused exploration, its purpose and sequence
- Gain basic understanding of the teacher's role during focused exploration
- Continue to build understanding of the science concepts and inquiry skills and how they are expressed in children's behaviors and conversation
- Begin to understand what children's exploration in focused exploration might look like
- Build deeper understanding of the difference between open exploration and focused exploration, as well as the transition between the two

OVERVIEW

- Discuss observations (30 minutes)
- A closer look at focused exploration (1 hour)

INSTRUCTOR PREPARATION

- **PREVIEW VIDEO VIGNETTE 4.** Prepare for using the video vignette by previewing it and identifying the key points you want to make about these children and their teacher. The vignette highlights a girl who is focused on replicating a block structure from a picture in a book. Her challenge is finding the right placement of blocks at the base so that she can successfully build up. Vignette 5 shows children engaged in building enclosures and would also be useful when discussing focused exploration. Instructions for using vignette 5 are in advanced workshop 8, p. 90.

MATERIALS

- VCR, monitor, and video cued to vignette 4
- Overhead projector, screen, and overheads 5.1–5.3
- Copies of the vignette observation form and transcript to video vignette 4, and "Read and Reflect 6"
- Chart: "The Teacher's Role"

Activity

DISCUSS OBSERVATIONS (30 MINUTES)

PURPOSE: Provide another opportunity for sharing experiences, addressing issues that have surfaced, and encouraging collaboration between teachers.

Facilitate sharing classroom experiences using these questions to guide the conversation: (You might show overhead 1.2: "Inquiry Diagram" and 1.3: "Science Concepts" during this conversation.)

- What inquiry skills have children been using? Probe for specific evidence to support their statements.

- What science concepts are your children exploring?

- How do you plan to encourage further inquiry and promote deeper science understandings? Spend some time helping them think about this, using the teacher's guide as a reference.

> You might want to collect and review teachers' observations and reflections. You will get a sense of how well they understand the workshop content. You will also get ideas for follow-up.

A CLOSER LOOK AT FOCUSED EXPLORATION (1 HOUR)

PURPOSE: This interactive activity will familiarize teachers with focused exploration, its purpose and its flow. They will gain a deeper understanding of young children's inquiry and what it looks like in the classroom. A vignette showing a teacher and children building is used to illustrate what focused exploration looks like in a classroom.

1. **PROVIDE OVERVIEW OF FOCUSED EXPLORATION USING THREE OVERHEADS.** (Take no more than 30 minutes for this.) Refer teachers to the "Focused Exploration" section of the teacher's guide. Tell them that you are going to help them understand the purpose and flow of activity, their role as a teacher, and what children's focused exploration might look like.

   a. Introduce focused exploration by reviewing overhead 5.1.

OVERHEAD 5.1: PURPOSE OF FOCUSED EXPLORATION

- **Give children opportunities to investigate specific questions in depth**
  The term "focused" refers to the investigation of a particular question or idea about building. The term "investigation" implies that the children are deepening their use of inquiry through prediction, planning, data collection, and analysis. Children's understandings grow as they pursue their own particular interests and questions.

- **Give children the support, materials, and time they need to deepen their exploration**
  Whether in open or focused exploration, time, materials, and support are always key to inquiry-based science. Remember that the teacher's role as a guide is key when it is time to engage in the more advanced skills of inquiry like data collection and analysis.

Help teachers to make connections to their experiences in the last exploration by asking, "What specific activities did you engage in during the towers exploration that would exemplify focused exploration?" Question further by asking, "How was that different from being engaged in open exploration?"

   b. Show overhead 5.2 and review the elements of focused exploration for building towers and enclosures. Refer the teachers to p. 13 in the "Getting Ready" section of the teacher's guide during this conversation.

Overhead 5.2: Elements of Focused Exploration

- **Exploration focuses on building towers and enclosures**
  These two challenges, towers and enclosures, present different issues when working to achieve strength and stability. One presents the challenge of building height and the other building walls, roofs, and apertures (openings for doors or windows). Explorations focused on these challenges provide an experiential base from which children develop ideas about forces, design, and materials.

- **Walkabouts are used as a strategy for sharing and analyzing buildings**
  At the end of choice time there is an opportunity to share what has been done before the buildings have to come down. This is a perfect time to do some reflecting on what has gone on that day. Conversations can review achievements and the strategies used while viewing the results. It is an important time to build community knowledge about structures, materials, strength, and stability.

- **Books, posters, neighborhood walks, and visiting experts are used to stimulate building and thinking**
  Children's motivation and ideas about their work are fueled by seeing a variety of buildings, learning about the roles of people associated with building, and seeing the tools of their work (such as an architect's blueprints).

- **Two- and three-dimensional representation is used to reflect on work**
  The process of drawing or creating a three-dimensional representation refocuses children on what they have done, encourages close examination, and offers new challenges as they change medium.

- **Science talks are used to share experiences and ideas**
  Regular conversations provide opportunities to share building experiences, successful strategies, and theories about why buildings are staying up or falling down. Children learn from each other and bring new insight into their next building experiences.

---

c. Use overhead 5.3 to discuss the transition from open to focused exploration. (Refer them to p. 33 in the teacher's guide.) Connect these points back to comments they made when discussing their observations. Help them understand who in their classrooms is showing signs of being ready to focus.

Overhead 5.3: The Transition from Open to Focused

Look for children to do the following:

- **Spend a full choice time building purposefully**
  You may see children choosing the block area at the beginning of choice time and remaining there. They may connect their play from one day to the next by building bridges repeatedly, or just enjoy exploring what the blocks can do.

- **Become deliberate in how they build their structures**
  As children place one block next to another, they may have an idea of how they want them to fit together. They may purposefully rearrange blocks to get more stability or better balance.

- **Choose to build regularly**
  Do you see the same children in the block area or other building centers day after day?

Connect these ideas to those on overhead 5.1 by sharing that these children are engaged in inquiry by exploring important ideas about forces, the characteristics of materials, and elements of design that influence balance and stability. Their exploration and emerging questions reflect the beginning of investigation. They are already focused on building as an activity—now is the time to focus them on the science of what they are doing.

2. **VIEW AND DISCUSS VIGNETTE 4** (20 minutes). Introduce the vignette by saying that it was taped in a Boston kindergarten and focuses on two children building with Kapla blocks at a table. Explain to teachers that they will view the vignette twice.

   a. Before the first viewing, distribute the transcript. Tell teachers to note the children's engagement and learning as they watch the vignette. You might refer them to the teacher's guide chart of outcomes and review it before starting the video. Show the vignette and then let them share their comments for a few minutes.

   b. Prepare them for the second viewing of the video by giving each teacher a copy of the vignette observation form. Ask them to examine the role the teacher plays this time and note their observations in the teacher column of the form. They can also note additional observations about the children.

   c. Show the video and give them a few minutes to record observations and thoughts.

   d. Bring groups together and guide a discussion using the following questions:

   • Why would you characterize this vignette as a focused exploration? Probe for specific examples.

   • This teacher played a key role in the children's experience. What did she do to encourage engagement and guide inquiry?

   • What might the next step be for these children?

You may want to highlight the following points when discussing vignette 4.

Look for ideas like these about the children's engagement and focused exploration:

- Jessica is engaged in a focused investigation—she replicates the photograph of a block building that is "difficult" to build. Her deliberate actions reflect her readiness to focus her work. Careful observation of her actions and their effect provides data for analysis.

- Jessica and Arthur reflect some analysis skill when they talk about easy and hard building challenges.

- Note the difference in how blocks are placed in these three structures. Jessica places hers on end, and Arthur and Olan place theirs flat.

- Arthur is less adventuresome. He first works on an "easy structure" before helping Jessica.

Look for these ideas about the role the teacher plays:

- Jessica asks for the teacher's help, who responds by coming and sitting with her. She focuses Jessica's attention to the spacing of the blocks with questions. She reflects back with Jessica about what she is doing with questions like, "Why are you pushing them out like that?"

- Asks for a prediction and gives language to the possible outcomes, "Will it get *wider* or *closer*?" Without solving the problem, she helps Jessica reflect and determine how to proceed.

Look for these ideas about possible next steps:

- The teacher could encourage Jessica to go further with her inquiry. She might do two- and three-dimensional representations that can be used to share the work with others. She might be challenged to try the structure with different materials and compare the experiences. The teacher might suggest that Jessica figure out how to add a roof or door to the structure.

- Find ways to engage Arthur in more of the inquiry (such as taking more risks in his building, predicting outcomes, and reflecting on his work). Pushing for more input from him might lead to interesting conversations if he and Jessica differ in their opinions about something.

3. **IN CONCLUSION,** refer teachers again to "The Teacher's Roles," p. 73 in "Resources" in the teacher's guide. They will find further description of strategies to use during focused exploration here. Collect "Read and Reflect 5" and distribute "Read and Reflect 6." Remind teachers of the time and place for the next workshop.

BASIC WORKSHOP 5: VIGNETTE OBSERVATION FORM

Name: _____

VIEWING 1	VIEWING 2
Observe: • Types of play • Abilities and interests • Experiences with science concepts	Observe: • Teacher strategies

TRANSCRIPT OF VIDEO VIGNETTE 4: FOCUSED EXPLORATION WITH KAPLAS

Scene: In this Boston kindergarten, three children—Arthur, Jessica, and Olan—are working with Kaplas at a table.

Jessica: Not that crooked. Okay, this is the last one. Okay, now we have to go back *(points at picture on table)*. Oh, no, it's hard.

Arthur: No way. Not for me.

Olan: Yeah, doing the—that's the last easy one.

Jessica: That's so easy. We're not doing that one. We're making hard ones. Right, Arthur?

Arthur: *(Puts Kaplas side by side and builds on top in same direction.)* This is how you make the easy ones. Look, this is how you make the easy ones.

Jessica: Yeah.

Arthur: This is the easy one. This is the easy one.

Jessica: Then that.

Arthur: No, not yet.

(Background chatter)

Arthur: This is the way they make the easy ones. We're making hard ones.

(Background chatter)

Jessica: Mrs.—I need some help with this—to make that one.

Teacher: Oh, okay. So what are you trying to make—a square or what?

Unknown: Arthur, I need some of those blocks.

Arthur: You need some what?

Unknown: Are you making your own thing?

Teacher: Does that look like—?

Jessica: No.

Unknown: Because I need some of those blocks.

Teacher: Something's—

Jessica: Ay-yay, yay!

Teacher: Okay, who has the right . . . Okay, that's . . . Now, what do you have to do? You have to make sure they have enough?

Jessica: Space.

Teacher: Right.

Unknown: Don't you *(inaudible)*? Jessica, why you take it away from me? *(Arthur is helping Jessica with her structure.)*

Teacher: Now see how—Arthur, see how wide this is? This is what I was talking about. So what do you think?

Jessica: I do not know.

Teacher: Why [are] you pushing them out like that?

Jessica: Oh.

Teacher: Ah, ah—Olan, no. Don't take his. Okay.

Unknown: I'm losing these.

Teacher: Now look—Jessica, look at this. Look at this space in between here and the space in between here. Is that the same? Huh? *(Jessica shakes her head no.)* So what do you think is going to happen?

Arthur: I think this is going to fall.

Teacher: Why?

Arthur: I don't know. *(Arthur and Jessica are continuing to build their "hard" structure.)*

Teacher: What do you think, Jessica? What do you think? The more space you have here—

Jessica: The less space we have here?

Teacher: Is it going to make it wider or is it going to make it—

Jessica: Lower?

Teacher: Closer?

Jessica: Closer.

Teacher: Closer? The more space you have? *(Both children continue to build up on structure.)*

Unknown: *(Inaudible)* cleaned up.

Jessica: No, we have to save it.

Jessica: I'm saving it.

READ AND REFLECT 6:
FOCUSED EXPLORATION

Name: _____

Observe a small group of children (two to four) engaged in focused exploration, and complete an observation record (p. 93 in the teacher's guide). Respond to these questions as you reflect on what you observed.

1. What characterizes this activity as focused exploration?

2. What science inquiry skills were the children using? Refer to the science outcomes chart in the teacher's guide and make specific connections between the skills listed and children's comments and behaviors.

3. What science concepts were the children exploring? Refer to the outcomes chart and make specific connections between the concepts listed and your children's comments and behaviors.

4. What might be appropriate next steps for these children? Please explain how each idea will encourage further inquiry and promote deeper science understandings. Refer to specific steps in the teacher's guide.

5. How would you rate the quality of your observation notes? Did you record descriptive details that were useful when reflecting? What might you want to do differently next time?

Focused Exploration of Enclosures

AT A GLANCE

Purpose:

- Engage in a focused exploration of enclosures
- Deepen understanding of the science concepts and inquiry skills
- Extend understanding of the teacher's role as a facilitator of focused exploration

Activity	Time	Materials
Discuss Observation Facilitate a brief exchange of teachers' observations from focused exploration.	20 minutes	• "Read and Reflect 6"
Focused Exploration of Building Enclosures Facilitate a focused exploration by engaging teachers in the challenges of building enclosures. Model the teacher's role by encouraging inquiry and engagement with the science concepts.	1 hour and 15 minutes	• A variety of building materials, including roofing materials • Props • Sample books with photos of enclosures • Materials for two-dimensional representation • Chart: "Strategies for Building Enclosures" • Copies of "Basic Workshop Evaluation"

Preassignment: Complete "Read and Reflect 6," conducting an observation and responding to the reflection questions.

Workshop 6: Focused Exploration of Enclosures

OBJECTIVES

- Engage in a focused exploration of building enclosures
- Deepen understanding of the science concepts and inquiry skills
- Extend understanding of the teacher's role as a facilitator of focused exploration

OVERVIEW

- Discuss observations (20 minutes)
- Focused exploration of building enclosures (1 hour 15 minutes)

INSTRUCTOR PREPARATION

- **REVIEW THE ENCLOSURES SECTION OF FOCUSED EXPLORATION.** With the steps from the teacher's guide fresh in your mind, you can make valuable connections to what participants will be doing with children.
- **SET UP A BUILDING ENVIRONMENT WITH ENCLOSURE MATERIALS.** If you are going to have participants work on tables, use small blocks such as Kapla, mini unit, and so on. Be sure there are enough for each group of three or four participants. Place one or two books with photos of enclosed spaces near building areas. Ideally you will have floor space for the unit blocks and other larger building materials as well.

MATERIALS

- "Read and Reflect 6"
- A variety of building materials, including roofing materials (such as pieces of cardboard in different sizes, roof board, and oak tag)
- Props of living things that can go inside enclosures (such as plastic animals, dolls, cars, and so on)
- Sample photo books that show enclosures (such as houses with visible windows, a garage, or a stadium)
- Materials for two-dimensional representation: pencils, rulers, and drafting tools
- Chart: "Strategies for Building Enclosures," with three columns: "Roofs and Floors," "Doors and Windows," and "Walls"
- Copies of "Basic Workshop Evaluation"

Activity

DISCUSS OBSERVATIONS (20 MINUTES)

PURPOSE: As teachers share their experiences, you will have a chance to encourage collaboration and ongoing dialogue about science teaching. You will also be able to identify issues that need addressing.

Facilitate a conversation in which teachers share their recent experiences with focused exploration. You might use questions like these:

- What inquiry skills have you seen children using? Ask for specific evidence to support their statements.

- What science concepts are children in your classroom exploring? Again, ask for specifics.

- How do you plan to encourage further inquiry and promote deeper science understandings? Spend some time helping them think about this. Use the teacher's guide as a reference.

- What kinds of dramatic play (if at all) do the children engage in when they are building? Dramatic play might not occur as much for children engaged in building towers, but others might be making buildings for a specific purpose (fire stations, houses for dolls, and so on). This information will relate directly to the following focused exploration.

> You might want to collect and review their observation and reflection. You will get a sense of how well they are understanding the workshop content and get ideas for follow-up.

FOCUSED EXPLORATION OF BUILDING ENCLOSURES (1 HOUR 15 MINUTES)

PURPOSE: This activity will help the teachers deepen their understanding of focused exploration as it applies to enclosures, and learn more about how to use children's dramatic play to deepen their science understandings.

1. **INTRODUCE THE ACTIVITY** (5 minutes) by telling teachers about the next focused exploration. Similar in format to workshop 4, this exploration will be about enclosed spaces.

2. **PROCESS THEIR INITIAL REACTIONS** (10 minutes). Ask teachers to think about examples of building enclosures, which might include windows, doors, rooms, or roofs. You might ask, "What kinds of building issues do you think will arise when trying to build a garage for a car, or a house with a roof for an animal? How are these issues the same as or different from those encountered in building towers?" As you listen to teachers' responses, ask for specifics.

Although they are still experiencing forces while working to create stability and balance, there are new issues to consider:

- Creating walls that stand up

- Designing a roof and selecting the right materials

- Building a roof with a span across open space

- Focusing on multiple characteristics, rather than just one (such as height)

3. **INTRODUCE THE ENCLOSURES CHALLENGE** (5 minutes). Show teachers the various props (such as plastic animals, dolls, toy cars) you brought. Ask them to imagine they are involved in building structures for these props that have some inside space, so the props can move around, be protected from rain, look outside, get in and out, and so on. Ask them to think about how they will build to provide some of these enclosed spaces. Show teachers the building materials that will be available, including the new materials you brought for roofing. Suggest that they might refer to the books to get ideas for enclosed spaces.

4. **BUILD ENCLOSURES** (25 minutes). Encourage teachers to start building enclosures with the materials in the building center. Tell them that they will draw representations of their structure later.

   a. As you visit each group, model the teacher's role in the following ways:

   - Restate the original challenge. ("Remember to try to provide inside space for your prop.")

   - Give positive encouragement. ("This is an interesting indoor space with a lot of area.")

   - Ask questions about the materials they are using or the building challenges they are facing. ("What did you have to do in order to make enough space for the car?" "What did you have to keep in mind to make a roof?" "How might you build a door?")

   - Offer additional challenges. ("Can you build a second floor for this person's house? How will she get up the stairs? How will she look out?")

   b. Near the end of the building time, have teachers draw their enclosures.

   c. Allow at least five minutes for teachers to walk around the room to observe other teachers' structures. Encourage them to talk with each other about the building challenges they faced.

5. **DISCUSS ENCLOSURES** (20 minutes). Gather teachers together to talk about the strategies they used when faced with building different kinds of enclosures.

   a. On a chart labeled "Strategies for Building Enclosures" with three columns ("Roofs and Floors," "Doors and Windows," and "Walls"), list responses under the appropriate headings.

   b. Try to ask questions that keep the focus on how those strategies relate to the science concepts.

Examples of responses and probing questions:

- Relationship to forces: gravity, tension, and compression—Ask questions and make comments that call attention to science concepts. For example, "How did you keep the roof from caving in?" "Were your walls able to support the roof?" "How did you keep the wall strong even though there is a window?"

- Certain designs are stronger and more stable—"What designs made your wall more stable?" "What was important about how you made windows and doors?"

- Different materials have different purposes—"What materials seemed to make good roofs? Why?"

6. **DISCUSS THE TEACHER'S ROLE** (10 minutes). Say something like this: "I have been leading you through a challenge about building with enclosed spaces. What have I been doing and why?" Help the participants develop understanding by asking questions like these:

   - "How have I tried to keep you within your dramatic play settings?" (You are looking for them to identify ways in which you have used their dramatic play settings to keep them focused on specific science concepts—forces, stability and balance, characteristics of materials, elements of design.)

   - "Can you relate to what we've been doing to the inquiry process?"

   - "How has this challenge of building enclosed spaces provided experiences with the science concepts?"

7. **IN CONCLUSION,** distribute the basic workshop evaluation and have teachers complete it, if time allows, or arrange to collect it later. Let the teachers know how you will be following up and supporting their implementation of the teacher's guide.

BASIC WORKSHOP EVALUATION

Name (optional): _____

1. To what degree have the workshops helped you learn about these topics:

    The science of building

    □————□————□————□————□
    not at all   *adequate*   *significant*

    Science teaching

    □————□————□————□————□
    not at all   *adequate*   *significant*

    Using the teacher's guide

    □————□————□————□————□
    not at all   *adequate*   *significant*

2. Overall, I found the level of challenge to be:

    □————□————□————□————□
    not at all   *appropriately*   *much too*
    challenging   *challenging*   *challenging*

    Please explain:

3. Overall, I found the workshops to be valuable to my science teaching:

    □————□————□————□————□
    not at all   *valuable*   *extremely*
    valuable   *valuable*

    Please explain:

4. To what extent have you already applied learning from the workshops to your work?

    □————□————□————□————□
    no   *some*   *extensive*
    application   *application*   *application*

    Please describe one approach that has had the greatest effect on children's learning:

5. What new insights have you gained about teaching an inquiry-based science curriculum?
   Please explain your answer (be specific):

6. What new insights have you gained about *your role* in relation to young children's science learning?

7. What do you suggest we do differently next time?

Building Structures with Young Children guiding principles

- Three- to five-year-olds can experience rich, in-depth, scientific inquiry.

- Science content draws from children's experiences, is interesting and engaging, and can be explored directly and deeply over time.

- Expectations are developmentally appropriate.

- Discussion, expression, and representation are critical ways in which children reflect on and develop theories from their active work.

- Children learn from one another.

- Teachers can take on specific roles that actively support and guide children's science learning.

INQUIRY

Engage, notice, wonder, question

Focus observations, clarify questions

Plan, predict,
take action

Ask new
questions

Explore, investigate

Observe
closely

Reflect on experience,
explore patterns and
relationships, construct
reasonable explanations

Collect, record, represent
experiences and data

**Share, discuss, and reflect with group;
draw conclusions; formulate ideas
and theories**

SCIENCE CONCEPTS

- Forces: gravity, tension, and compression

- Certain designs are stronger and more stable

- Different building materials have different characteristics

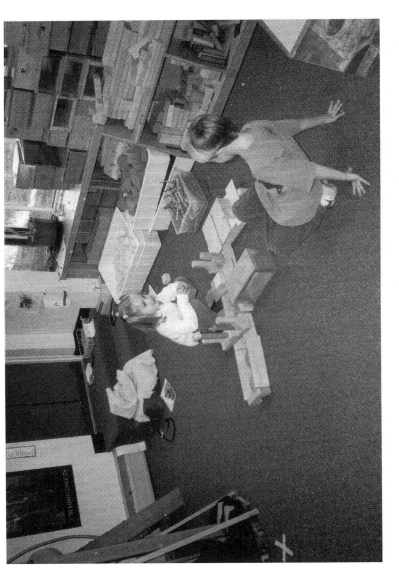

How does this environment encourage building structures?

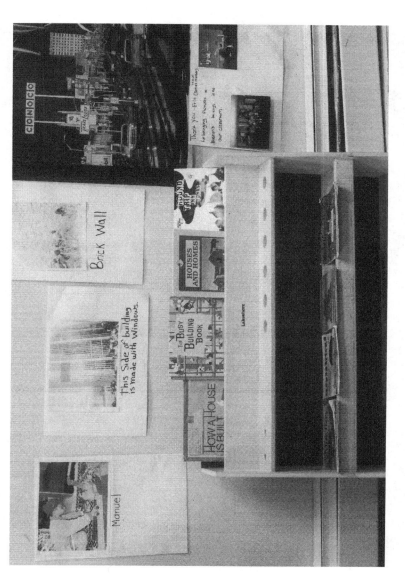

How does this environment encourage building structures?

How does this environment encourage building structures?

How does this environment encourage building structures?

TYPES OF BLOCK PLAY

- Constructive

- Dramatic and symbolic

- Exploratory

INFLUENCE ON BLOCK PLAY

- Previous experience
- Culture
- Development

Purpose of Open Exploration

- To give children opportunities to wonder about, notice, and explore

- To give children the support, materials, and time they need to begin their exploration

FLOW OF OPEN EXPLORATION

- Step 1: Introduce children to building structures

- Step 2: Ongoing exploration and reflections

PURPOSE OF FOCUSED EXPLORATION

- To give children opportunities to investigate specific questions in more depth

- To give children the support, materials, and time they need to deepen their exploration

ELEMENTS OF FOCUSED EXPLORATION

- Exploration focuses on building towers and enclosures

- Walkabouts are used as a strategy for sharing and analyzing buildings

- Books, posters, neighborhood walks, and visiting experts are used to stimulate building and thinking

- Two- and three-dimensional representation is used to reflect on work

- Science talks are used to share experiences and ideas

The Transition from Open Exploration to Focused Exploration

Look for children doing the following:

- Spending a full choice time building purposefully

- Becoming deliberate in how they build their structures

- Choosing to build regularly

advanced workshops

Overview

The eight advanced workshops are designed to build teachers' ability to engage children in scientific inquiry. Although the workshops are numbered, they are in no particular order. However, you may want to start with workshop 7: "Creating a Culture of Inquiry about Building Structures." In this workshop, teachers assess their skills as science teachers. The results can help you create a sequence of workshops that responds to the interests and needs of teachers. All of the ninety-minute workshops use an instructional approach that encourages application of new ideas. The presentation of new material is combined with activities that encourage teachers to apply what they are learning as they analyze classroom practice and children's work, and as they plan the next steps.

The advanced workshops include the following:

7. **CREATING A CULTURE OF INQUIRY ABOUT BUILDING STRUCTURES:** This workshop addresses the environment and climate of a classroom that encourages building, including strategies for conveying the excitement, challenge, and wonder that can occur when children build with many different materials. Teachers complete an evaluation of their skills as science teachers and develop individual goals for professional development.

8. **DEEPENING CHILDREN'S SCIENCE UNDERSTANDINGS:** In this workshop, teachers focus on the ways they can deepen children's science understandings by encouraging and guiding their inquiry.

9. **USING BOOKS TO EXTEND SCIENCE LEARNING:** This workshop helps teachers integrate books into their ongoing science exploration. The role, selection, and use of fiction and nonfiction books in an investigation of building will be covered.

10. **ASSESSING CHILDREN'S SCIENCE LEARNING:** In this workshop, teachers discuss young children's science learning—the outcomes they might expect, how to document engagement and learning, and how they can use their documentation to plan their next steps.

11. **Encouraging Representation:** This workshop addresses the importance of representation. Strategies for encouraging children to use varied media to communicate their observations and understandings are discussed.

12. **Using Children's Representations as Teaching Tools:** This workshop draws on knowledge and skills built in workshop 11: "Encouraging Representation" by helping teachers use children's work to deepen their science understanding.

13. **Facilitating Science Talks:** This workshop provides teachers with strategies for facilitating successful large and small group science talks, often considered the most difficult aspect of science teaching.

14. **Making and Using Documentation Panels:** This workshop takes teachers through the process of making panels and addresses how these panels can be used as a springboard for stimulating discussions, reenactments, and further exploration.

Assignments

Each advanced workshop has a preassignment. Preassignments include readings in the teacher's guide; reflection questions; and gathering materials, such as children's work, to discuss in the workshop. These assignments prepare teachers for participating fully in workshop discussions and activities. Be sure to distribute them at least one week before the workshop, emphasizing their importance.

Advanced Workshop Instructions

The instructions for each workshop follow the same format as the basic workshops. Each workshop includes the following sections:

- At a Glance outlines the purpose, activities, timeline, materials, and preassignment for each session

- Objectives identify what skills you want teachers to gain by the end of the session

- An overview describes the activities and how much time to devote to each one

- Instructor Preparation lists the materials you need and how to prepare for each session

- Detailed step-by-step instructions provide guidance for leading each activity

- Handouts to copy for each participant

- Overheads to copy as transparencies before each session

- "Read and Reflect" preassignments to copy and distribute at least a week before each workshop

Handouts, overheads, or assignments appear after most workshop's instructions. You will also find suggested next steps, which offers ideas that help teachers with follow-up, as they apply their new learnings to their classrooms.

"Next Steps" include the following:

- Strategy handouts: In many workshops, teachers develop lists of strategies they have found useful, read about in the teacher's guide, or seen in vignettes. Type up strategies and distribute them.

- Plan another workshop: Choose one that builds on the skills teachers are developing. Be sure that teachers have time to work with the content of at least one workshop before offering another. We suggest one-month intervals.

- Plan guided conversations: Focused conversation in small groups is an excellent way for teachers to deepen their understandings and build their ability, once the content has been presented. Help teachers create relevant documents from their classrooms to use as material that stimulates thought and discussion. For example, videotaped or audiotaped science talks would make excellent documents for discussion after workshop 13. Transcribing is a great idea as well.

- Mentoring: Individual support may be the best way to support teachers. Careful examination of teachers' work supports reflective practice, while giving you the insights needed to tailor your approach based on teachers' interests and needs.

- Recommended reading: The bibliography is full of valuable books and articles. Distribute these to teachers at strategic points during the workshop. Be sure to use this material to build your understanding of science teaching and learning as well.

Creating a Culture of Inquiry about Building Structures

AT A GLANCE

Purpose:

- Build strategies for creating a culture of inquiry about building structures
- Assess knowledge and skills as science teachers
- Set goals for professional development as science teachers

Activity	Time	Materials
Define term "culture of inquiry" Present characteristics of a culture of inquiry and use a video vignette to illustrate your points.	40 minutes	• Chart: "Strategies for Creating a Culture of Inquiry" • VCR, monitor, and video cued to vignette 1 • Overhead projector, screen, and overhead 7.1
Complete the self-assessment Engage teachers in completing the "Evaluating Science Teaching" form (p. 207). Facilitate small group discussion of needs and goals.	35 minutes	• Copies of "Evaluating Science Teaching"
Conduct collective goal setting Have groups share their goals and issues, and make plans for supporting further professional development.	15 minutes	• Copies of small group recording form • Charts: "Our Strengths as Science Teachers" and "Our Needs as Science Teachers"

Preassignment: Read the introduction to the teacher's guide.

Advanced Workshop 7: Creating a Culture of Inquiry about Building Structures

OBJECTIVES

- Build strategies for creating a culture of inquiry about building structures
- Assess knowledge and skills as science teachers
- Set goals for professional development as science teachers

OVERVIEW

- Define term "culture of inquiry" (40 minutes)
- Complete self-assessment (35 minutes)
- Conduct collective goal setting (15 minutes)

INSTRUCTOR PREPARATION

- **ASSIGN READING.** At least one week before the workshop, ask teachers to read the introduction to *Building Structures with Young Children* teacher's guide.

- **CONSIDER OBSERVING TEACHERS IN THE CLASSROOM AT THIS TIME.** This will give you valuable information about teachers' science teaching. Start by deciding which parts of the "Evaluating Science Teaching" form you want to use. If the teachers are beginners, it might not be appropriate for them to use the whole form. As teachers become more skilled you will want to expand the aspects of their practice that you are focusing on. Use the following when planning your observations:

    - When evaluating beginning teachers, focus on sections I A, B, and C; section II A1, A2, and B1.

    - When evaluating developing teachers, focus on the sections that you used for the beginning teacher and add section I D and the rest of section II.

    - When evaluating teachers who are refining their skills, use the whole form.

- **PREVIEW VIGNETTE 1.** Look at the vignette, being sure that you understand the points that should be made.

MATERIALS

- 3 charts: "Strategies for Creating a Culture of Inquiry," "Our Strengths as Science Teachers," and "Our Needs as Science Teachers"
- VCR, monitor, and video cued to vignette 1
- Overhead projector, screen, and overhead 7.1
- Copies of evaluating science teaching (p. 207 in resources) and small group recording forms (one for each group)

Activity

DEFINE TERM "CULTURE OF INQUIRY" (40 MINUTES)

PURPOSE: To build a common understanding of the elements that contribute to a positive and productive climate for science learning.

1. **INTRODUCE THE WORKSHOP AND THE TERM "CULTURE OF INQUIRY"** (10 minutes). Give a quick overview of the workshop. Explain that one of the most important roles inquiry-based science teachers will play is to create a "culture of inquiry about building structures." This culture promotes children's investigation of building structures through use of varied materials and designs. In this environment, the physical space and the interactions convey the excitement and wonder of the building process. Review overhead 7.1, providing a quick overview of the elements of this culture. You will discuss them more in-depth after viewing the vignette.

OVERHEAD 7.1: THE CULTURE OF INQUIRY ABOUT BUILDING STRUCTURES

- **An emphasis on the importance of building structures**
  A building environment conveys the importance of building structures of all kinds. It emphasizes use of many kinds of blocks and building materials, and the challenge of building in different ways. The importance of building is conveyed through provision of time and space, selection and display of varied building materials, and displays that stimulate interest and reflect children's building experiences and ideas.

- **An emphasis on inquiry**
  Builders ask questions, observe closely over time, and think about what their observations tell them. The teacher's role is not to provide the answers, but to encourage the children to ask questions and support them as they seek answers. There is an emphasis on gathering data (or evidence) and recording it for reflection and analysis. The room is filled with children's work, photographs, charts, and panels that communicate the value of documentation.

- **Sharing observations and experiences**
  In a culture of inquiry, children are encouraged to share their building experiences and ideas through small and large group science talks, and they learn to listen to what others have to say. They share their records of what they have built or their ideas about science concepts, such as what makes a tower stable or how different kinds of building materials affect a structure's integrity. They learn that all ideas are valued, that people have different ideas, and that one can learn by asking questions of others.

- **Recording observations and ideas**
  Builders spend a great deal of time recording what they do—using careful sketches and descriptive words to most accurately remember their experiences. They use their records to reflect with others and find patterns in their explorations. Some builders may use drawing to help them plan as architects do. In a building environment, materials for representation are easily available and children's work is used to discuss their ideas and stimulate more focused investigations.

---

2. **USE VIGNETTE 1 TO ILLUSTRATE THESE POINTS** (30 minutes). Introduce the vignette, saying that they will be viewing the vignette they saw in basic workshop 1 again. Ask them to note the specific environmental and interaction strategies the teachers are using to create a culture of inquiry about building.

Show the vignette and then ask for comments. Project overhead 7.1 while you talk. Guide teachers to identify specific strategies and note them on your chart. Connect each to the characteristic (from 7.1) to which the strategy relates. Be sure their ideas include both environment and interaction strategies.

Look for ideas like these:

- Varied materials were available for building, allowing children to experience how different characteristics (size, texture, shape, weight) affect their structures.

- Clipboards with paper seemed easily accessible for representation.

- Teachers worked with the children in the block area at their level. Their presence validated the importance of their work and supported their efforts.

- Teachers' questions focused the children and helped them collect and analyze the details of their work.

- Teachers used representation and conversation to encourage reflection.

COMPLETE THE SELF-ASSESSMENT (35 MINUTES)

PURPOSE: While these key strategies are fresh in the teachers' minds, it will be important to help them think about the ones they need to build into their repertoire. This process will help you determine the content and form of professional development that will be most helpful to teachers right now.

1. **DISTRIBUTE "EVALUATING SCIENCE TEACHING"** to each teacher and ask them to take the next fifteen minutes to complete it. Emphasize the importance of openness. Remind the teachers that they all have strengths and weaknesses as teachers, but probably most are willing to acknowledge that science teaching is not a strength. The teachers' ability to examine their own work will be the first step toward building the kind of reflective practice that will support their development as science teachers.

   While they work, move around the room seeing that everyone is on task. Help them interpret items that might confuse them.

2. **AFTER FIFTEEN MINUTES, ASK TEACHERS TO WORK IN SMALL GROUPS,** synthesizing their evaluation information (20 minutes). Help teachers divide into groups of three or four and give each group a "Small Group Synthesis Form." Review the questions. Ask them to have a conversation and note their thoughts on the form as they talk. Suggest they have a note taker as well as someone who facilitates the conversation, ensuring they address all of the questions in the allotted time.

CONDUCT COLLECTIVE GOAL SETTING (15 MINUTES)

PURPOSE: This is an opportunity for you to collect some "data." Where do these teachers see their strengths and needs? Your responsiveness to their needs and interests will generate enthusiasm.

1. **BEGIN THE CONVERSATION BY FOCUSING ON THEIR STRENGTHS** (5 minutes). Quickly let each group share their thinking. In any group, the strengths and needs will vary from teacher to teacher, but look for themes, as well as for teachers who can support others in particular areas. Note their thoughts on the chart you prepared. You will want to refer to this information later.

2. **Now gather their thoughts about their needs** (10 minutes). Repeat the process. Be sure each group has a chance to share. If you have time, encourage them to think about the next steps. You might want to offer alternatives, such as attending workshops, participating in guided discussions, and mentoring. Finish by letting teachers know what they might expect and reiterate your expectations for their use of the curriculum.

Suggested Next Steps

- Make a handout of the strategies teachers listed and distribute it.

- Offer workshops that best address the teachers' needs and interests.

- Design guided discussions that best address the teachers' needs and interests.

- Meet with each teacher individually to go over their evaluation, set goals, and make professional development plans. See the mentoring section for suggestions. We recommend that you conduct an observation in each room and fill out your own evaluation form before meeting with individual teachers.

- Suggested reading from the references:

"Creating an Environment for Science in the Classroom," chapter 2 in *Doing What Scientists Do: Children Learn to Investigate Their World,* by E. Doris (Heinemann, 1991).

SMALL GROUP SYNTHESIS FORM

As a group, share your individual thoughts about your strengths and needs, and record them below. Note where there was common agreement and where there was a lot of difference.

Our strengths as science teachers include the following:

Our needs as science teachers include the following:

Areas we would like to develop first:

Deepening Children's Science Understandings

AT A GLANCE

Purpose:

- Build understanding of the strategies teachers can use to deepen science understandings as children engage in inquiry
- Apply these strategies to design the next steps for the teacher featured in the video vignette

Activity	Time	Materials
Provide overview of how young children learn science Provide a rationale for this teaching approach by discussing how young children learn science.	30 minutes	• Overhead projector, screen, and overheads 8.1–8.4
Identify strategies for deepening children's science understandings Use excerpts from a teacher's journal to identify strategies for deepening children's science understandings. Reinforce ideas about the transition from open to focused exploration that were introduced in the basic workshops.	25 minutes	• Overhead 5.3 • Chart: "Strategies for Deepening Children's Science Understandings"
Analyze video vignette Ask teachers to analyze the strategies used by the teacher in the video vignette. In small groups, ask teachers to develop the next steps the teacher might take.	40 minutes	• Overhead 1.2 • VCR, monitor, and video cued to vignette 5: "Building Enclosures" • Copies of transcript of vignette 5 and vignette observation form

Preassignment: Read "The Teacher's Role" in resources (see p. 75) and "Building High: Excerpts from a Teacher's Journal" (see p. 10), both in the teacher's guide. Complete reflection questions.

Advanced Workshop 8:
Deepening Children's Science Understandings

OBJECTIVES

- Build understanding of the strategies teachers can use to deepen science understandings as children engage in inquiry

- Apply these strategies and design the next steps for the teacher featured in the video vignette

OVERVIEW

- Provide overview of how young children learn science (30 minutes)

- Identify strategies for deepening children's science understandings (25 minutes)

- Analyze video vignette (40 minutes)

INSTRUCTOR PREPARATION

- **ASSIGN "READ AND REFLECT."** Distribute "Read and Reflect 8" at least one week before the workshop.

- **PREVIEW VIGNETTE 5.** Watch the vignette and understand how it illustrates the points you want to make.

MATERIALS

- Overhead projector, screen, and overheads 1.2, 5.3, and 8.1–8.4

- VCR, monitor, and video cued to vignette 5: "Building Enclosures"

- Copies of handouts: transcript of vignette 5, vignette observation form, and "Read and Reflect 8"

- Chart: "Strategies for Deepening Children's Science Understandings," with two sections ("Encourage Exploration" and "Deepen Science Understanding")

Activity

OVERVIEW OF HOW YOUNG CHILDREN LEARN SCIENCE (30 MINUTES)

PURPOSE: To set the stage for the content that follows, building the connection between inquiry and its role in science learning with what we know about how young children learn.

1. **INTRODUCE THE WORKSHOP** and provide a quick overview of the main goals of an inquiry-based teacher (5 minutes). After introducing the topic of the workshop, show overhead 8.1: "The Science Teacher's Goals." Share that inquiry is an aspect of the science content that the children are learning. The more they learn about the inquiry process the more it becomes a tool that they can use throughout their lives. Emphasize that the focus here is inquiry science and that this workshop will focus on the second and third goals—how

teachers can guide children's inquiry and deepen children's science understandings. Mention that this might seem obvious, but in practice it is very difficult and these workshops are all designed to help them accomplish these goals.

OVERHEAD 8.1: THE SCIENCE TEACHER'S GOALS

- **Encourage children to build structures**
- **Guide children's inquiry**
- **Deepen children's science understanding**

---

2. **PROVIDE OVERVIEW OF HOW CHILDREN LEARN SCIENCE** (20 minutes) using overhead 8.2. Make the point that the inquiry approach to teaching science is based on what we know about the nature of science, as well as what we know about how children learn. Use the references to excerpts from a teacher's journal to illustrate the points, or ask your teachers if they can make these connections.

SLIDE 8.2: SCIENCE TEACHING AND LEARNING

- **Young children develop ideas about science from their life experiences**
  In the October 24 entry, children share their ideas about building towers in a group meeting. Key to this process is that the teacher provides opportunities to talk and focuses the talk on science.

- **New experiences lead children to challenge previous naïve ideas**
  Children's approach to building by trial and error often reveals naïve ideas; for example, Alina's efforts to get cylinders to rest on the top of her building in the October 6 entry. The teacher guides her to try new approaches that, in the end, focus her attention on the importance of block shape in creating balance.

- **A balance between exploration and thinking, reasoning, and theorizing provides a strong basis for learning**
  The excerpts from a teacher's journal provide a picture of how this balance plays out over time. Repeated patterns of doing and talking can deepen children's understanding over time. When the teacher encourages inquiry, lifelong patterns for learning are established.

- **Inquiry that leads to science learning takes time**
  These journal entries provide an excellent example of the kind of time it takes for children to build new understandings through inquiry. The quality of the children's inquiry deepens with time. For example, the November 15 investigation of tower building was more complex than the one on October 18. They have identified successful materials, strategies for building tall, and informal and formal methods for measurement. Children gradually learn to use inquiry, becoming an integral aspect of their learning process.

- **With guidance, children have the ability to engage in all aspects of the inquiry process**
  Note in the journal entries that children question, conduct investigations, collect data through observation and measurement, communicate their ideas, and make reasonable explanations, but the teacher plays a key role in guiding this process.

---

3. **CONCLUDE BY MAKING KEY POINTS ABOUT THIS APPROACH** (5 minutes). Use overheads 8.3 and 8.4 to focus your comments.

OVERHEAD 8.3: KEY IDEAS ABOUT THIS APPROACH TO SCIENCE LEARNING

- **Building understanding of important science concepts is an appropriate goal for young children**
  It is clear, from the vignettes and from the children's work samples that were included in the workshops and teacher's guide, that young children are capable of learning science.

- **Children naturally form ideas about the world based on their life experiences**
  When building structures, children's ideas are often revealed through the ways they try to put the blocks together. Careful observation of their efforts will give you important ideas about what they think will work and what they are trying to do.

- **In inquiry-based science our role is to provide new experiences that can lead children to more sophisticated theories**
  Our goal is to provide new experiences that will contribute to the development of new, more reasoned understandings. In particular, we hope children will begin to use evidence (what they have observed) as they build their ideas of how the world works. Comments, questions, and challenges that reflect our understandings of what they are trying to accomplish in their building are helpful in this process.

OVERHEAD 8.4:

"Experience is not the best teacher. It sounds like heresy, but when you think about it, it's reflection on experience that makes it educational."

George Forman
Professor Emeritus, University of Massachusetts

As teachers view overhead 8.4, explain that you will help them think about their role in providing the right experiences, helping children focus on the science in those experiences, and guiding a meaningful reflection process.

IDENTIFY STRATEGIES FOR DEEPENING CHILDREN'S SCIENCE UNDERSTANDINGS (25 MINUTES)

PURPOSE: The analysis of excerpts from a teacher's journal will highlight strategies teachers can use to promote children's science understandings.

1. **ANALYZE EXCERPTS FROM A TEACHER'S JOURNAL TO IDENTIFY STRATEGIES** (15 minutes). Ask teachers for strategies they found in the journal entries, noting their responses on the chart you have prepared. Use the question about literacy and math to highlight where science provides opportunities to promote learning early literacy and math concepts. Ask for specifics about what the journal says and connect it to the strategy they have identified.

An important point: deeper understandings grow out of reflection, but they are only possible with carefully focused experiences that happen over time. Look for strategies like these:

Encourage children's exploration:

- Worked with small groups during open exploration (October 6)
- Used observations to identify children's questions and interests (October 6 and 18)
- Created an environment that encourages children to build (September 14)
- Showed interest in and value for block play (October 6)
- Provided a challenge based on observation of interest (October 18)
- Shared strategies to support building success; encouraged collaboration and involvement of reluctant builders (October 24)
- Provided journals in the block area to encourage representation (October 30)

Deepen children's science understandings:

- Guided Alina's investigations to focus her on the properties of the blocks and how shape affects stability and balance (October 6)
- Offered a challenge that focuses the children on the materials—their properties, limitations, and possibilities (October 18)
- Facilitated sharing science ideas, strategies for stability and strength (October 24)
- Used representations to focus children's observations of their buildings (October 30)
- Responded to a request for help by identifying the question being explored (November 15)
- Encouraged measurement of their towers as a way of gathering data about their work (October 30 and November 15)

Supported literacy and math development:

- The teacher builds children's capacity to use language to express their ideas, which is key to early literacy and science understanding. It would be good for this teacher to also write down the children's ideas and use this text in posters or books created for the children's reference.
- On September 14, the teacher placed books in the block area. Interest in building is a great reason to look at books, learning to use them as a reference for information and a stimulus for building ideas. She also placed clipboards and markers in the block area to encourage the children to represent their buildings. This representation work is symbol making, a basic literacy skill. The process of making shapes as they represent blocks (October 30) is a part of learning about geometry.
- On October 24, the teacher talks about documenting the children's ideas to make a documentation panel. In this process she is modeling writing and recording ideas for the children and providing them a valuable resource that will interest many of them in reading. What could be more interesting than reading their own words?
- The teacher hangs journals next to the blocks on October 30 in order to further encourage representation and in this case make a book.
- On October 30 and November 15, the children are measuring their structures using informal (comparing to height of people) and formal (counting) methods. Measurement is a math process. Creating charts of different towers and recording their measurements is a good idea.

2. DISCUSS THE TRANSITION FROM OPEN EXPLORATION TO FOCUSED EXPLORATION (10 minutes). Spend a few minutes reviewing overhead 5.3 and talking about the transition from open exploration to focused exploration. Use journal excerpts and teacher's classroom observations (examples in box below) to illustrate how children show their readiness to focus.

    a. Review overhead 5.3 from basic workshop 5.

OVERHEAD 5.3: THE TRANSITION FROM OPEN EXPLORATION TO FOCUSED EXPLORATION

Look for children:

- **Spending a full choice time building purposefully**
  For example, you will see children choosing the block area at the beginning of choice time and remaining there for most of it. They may connect their play from one day to the next or just enjoy exploring what the blocks can do.

- **Becoming deliberate in how they build their structures**
  For example, as they place one block next to another they have an idea of how they want them to fit together. They may purposefully rearrange blocks to get more stability or better balance.

- **Choosing to build regularly**
  For example, the same particular children are in the block area or other building centers day after day.

Look for connections to the journal entries like these:

- Repeated tower building reflects purposeful and deliberate work.

- Alina and Reuben appear in two previous entries, implying that they may be regular builders.

- The conversation on October 24 reflects ideas that have grown out of purposeful and deliberate work.

---

    b. If you have time, encourage teachers to share their classroom observations, pinpointing readiness to shift to focused exploration, or alternately, children who are not ready to make the shift. Time won't permit everyone to share, but you will want to keep the conversation going until you have a variety of examples and you think everyone has a clear understanding of child behavior that show a readiness for focused investigation.

ANALYSIS OF VIGNETTE (40 MINUTES)

PURPOSE: Analyzing classroom practice will help teachers make the transition from theory to practice. While the vignette shows one point in time, this activity will put these isolated events into a context of inquiry that will build over the course of days and weeks.

1. READ THE STRATEGIES LISTED ON THE POSTER (5 minutes). Ask teachers if they have anything to add after reading the section on the teacher's role. Add their specific strategies to the list. Suggest that they can look for these strategies in the vignette, as well as add new ones.

2. **Use vignette 5 to further discuss how to deepen science understandings** (20 minutes). Begin by noting that this vignette was filmed in the same classroom as in vignette 3 in basic workshop 3. It is a Boston Head Start classroom with twenty three- and four-year-olds. Teachers will see a group of three children: James, Aria, and Thalia. Aria's first language is Farsi, and Thalia's is Spanish—both are English language learners. Pass out the vignette observation form and tell teachers that you want them to notice the ways the teacher encourages inquiry in order to deepen children's science understandings. As you discuss their observations, put new strategies in the appropriate column ("Encourage Exploration" and "Deepen Science Understanding"). Ask teachers of second language learners to look for these strategies as well.

> Three children are working to build stable enclosures with Kapla blocks, and all three children create walls and a roof. Thalia's blocks are carefully placed on top of each other. James and Aria are less careful, but James straightens his out carefully. The structures become less stable when the children build on top of the roofs using the Kapla blocks on their short ends. Through this process they are learning about the effective ways to use these blocks, the ways that forces affect them, and design features that help with stability. They overdo the support of their walls by filling in the inside space, but James uses this same strategy effectively when he stacks the blocks to support his structure on top and it doesn't fall like Thalia's does.
>
> Look for ideas such as the following:
>
> - Encouraging close observation ("They look kind of the same. Aria has a lot of space in his.")
>
> - Encouraging reasoning ("Do you have to have those pieces to hold the house up? How come you're putting that, it looks like a wall, up?")
>
> - Predicting or challenging ("Is there any way you can build one with more space for people? I wonder if you can make it strong enough so a wiggle can't knock it down?")
>
> - Providing more time for answering questions
>
> - Examining reasons for selection of certain blocks used to fill the space
>
> - Probing for comparison of the structures

3. **Discuss the next steps the teacher might make to expand the children's inquiry** (15 minutes). Put the inquiry diagram on the overhead projector (overhead 1.2). Point to the circle that illustrates the cyclical nature of inquiry in focused exploration, saying you want them to think about this aspect of inquiry as they plan strategies for deepening children's science understanding. Use the following questions to guide a discussion:

- What were children's interests and questions?

    - The children seemed interested in building structures with walls and roofs. They are also exploring different ways to use Kapla blocks and what strategies they need to create stability with them. They seem to be watching each other and trying out ideas they see.

    - What science concepts are these interests related to? What science are we deepening?

    - They are exploring creating stability in a structure with walls and a roof, the need for stability in walls, and how they can go high with Kaplas.

- How might the teacher use inquiry to deepen understanding about one or more of these science concepts? (You might pick one to focus on, then move on to another if there is time.) Taking design for stability as an example, here are some ideas:

  - Have children draw pictures of their structures, capturing the outside and inside space in their drawings. Document with photographs or teachers' drawings, and write down ideas they express.

  - Use the representations and photographs to reflect on what they did. This conversation might focus on comparing the structures—walls and open spaces— for example, you might say, "Did your walls stand up before you put the blocks inside? Why did you put them there? What happened when you added the roof? Did it affect the walls? What do you think makes walls strong?"

  - Challenge children by asking them to predict what might happen or be different, and record the results. Possibilities include these: "James, do you think you could build this building without the inside blocks?" "How many blocks can you take out and still have it standing?" "I wonder if there would be a way to put a window in this wall?" "Can you build a building just like this with different materials?"

  - Share and discuss with the whole group, using documentation of what was done. Explore questions about the needed blocks, asking others to speak from their experience. Find out if they have questions for the builders.

Emphasize that deepening children's science understandings can't happen in one day, but can take place over a week or two. Remind your teachers of the importance of documentation so they can build on children's experiences from one day to the next. For example, use children's representations of buildings or your photographs as a springboard for discussion—focus on stability and walls.

In closing, encourage teachers to continue sharing what they are doing in their classrooms. Remind them when and where the next workshop or guided discussion is and what they need to do to prepare.

Suggested Next Steps

- Make a handout of the strategies teachers have listed and distribute it.

- Follow up with teachers: Ask if they have any issues with focused exploration or with their role as a facilitator of inquiry. You may ask, "What are children's current interests and questions? How do they show these?"

Do teachers find ways to help children collect and record their data and talk about what it means?

- Offer the workshops on science talks or on representation as a way of extending the conversation about inquiry and deepening understanding.

- Guide a few discussions on these concepts. Record video vignettes in teachers' rooms to use for discussion. Help them consider next steps and plan ways to support how children collect and analyze data.

- Suggest readings from the following references:

Cooperative Problem Solving in the Classroom: Enhancing Young Children's Cognitive Development, by Jonathan Trudge and David Caruso (NAEYC, 1988)

Using Photographs to Support Children's Science Inquiry, by Cynthia Hoisington (NAEYC, 2002)

TRANSCRIPT OF VIDEO VIGNETTE 5:
BUILDING ENCLOSURES

Scene: Three children—James, Thalia, and Aria—are building enclosures with Kapla blocks on a table.

Aria: Ahh!

Thalia: Mine's going to fall. Look!

James: Make one like mine.

Thalia: Mine is little.

Unidentified child: What are you doing *(inaudible)*?

James: Mine and Thalia's . . .

Thalia: *(Inaudible)* I made it little. Mine *(sound of blocks falling)*. Oh!

Unidentified child: Oh.

Thalia: Aria, stop moving the blocks. You're making a mess.

James: You make a mess.

Thalia: We've got to look right up, like a little bit *(inaudible)*.

Aria: Look what I did.

Unidentified child: Guess what I did?

Unidentified child: Oh, that's—that's beautiful, but mine is like this way, and it has different stuff.

James: Now mine is better.

Teacher: Oh, what [are] you doing over here? You're working with Kaplas. Kaplas are challenging. Is that open in there? Can people go inside there?

Thalia: Yes.

Teacher: Tell me about this.

Thalia: That's a—that's a house.

Teacher: It's a house!

James: I'll tell you about mine. Aria, don't tell about *(inaudible)*.

Teacher: It looks like you're kind of making—they look kind of the same, like Thalia's looks kind of like James's, and Thalia's looks kind of like [Aria's] too.

Aria: Let me take, like this.

Teacher: Do you have to have those pieces to hold your house up?

Thalia: Yes.

Teacher: You do? Where do the people go, when they go inside?

Thalia: Go in here. *(Points)*

Teacher: Oh, right in that little—little alleyway there?

James: They all go in this way for mine.

Teacher: How do they go in yours, James? Can I look inside yours?

James: No. It's too small.

Teacher: It's too narrow? Too small? It's a tiny, narrow spot? Is there any way that you can build it with a little more space for the people to go inside?

James: How can I?

Teacher: I don't know. I'm wondering. Can I look inside it? *(Sound of blocks falling)* Oop, not now I can't.

Aria: From here.

Teacher: Oh, from this side I can? Okay. Oh, wow. Aria has a lot of space in his. Did you see it, Thalia?

Thalia: Yes.

Teacher: Can I move these out of the way so we can see it better?

Teacher: Aria, look at the space inside Thalia's.

Aria: We can put one up here.

Teacher: Aria is filling in your space inside.

Thalia: Okay. *(Inaudible)*

Teacher: I wanted to see if Thalia could take some out to make more space for the people.

James: Mine's better than Aria's.

Teacher: Tell me about what you're doing on the top over there.

James: I can't tell.

Teacher: You can't tell? Thalia is doing it too. How come you're putting these kind up, next to that part?

James: And why is she copying—copying me?

Teacher: Yes, she is. I think—are you copying [James's]?

Thalia: *(Inaudible)*

Teacher: Do you need more? *(Sound of blocks falling)* James, how come you're putting that—it looks like a wall up next to your . . .

James: *(Inaudible)* Aria.

Teacher: Well, it's hard not to wiggle the table when you're working on the table. Fine. I wonder if you can build something that's strong enough, so a little wiggle won't knock it down?

Aria: I've got one.

Teacher: You have to make it strong enough, so a little wiggle won't knock it down.

Teacher: Hmm.

Child: It looks dumb.

Teacher: Wow. You're doing something interesting. You're putting them that way? And now you're putting them the opposite way? You're putting them that way? *(Points to show the direction of the blocks.)*

James: Stop *(inaudible)* on the table, Aria.

Thalia: *(Sounds of blocks falling)* Oops!

Teacher: Uh, oh! James, I don't think your structure is—is very sturdy. I think you need to think about making it stronger.

Aria: You can put your feet like here.

ADVANCED WORKSHOP 8: VIGNETTE OBSERVATION FORM

Note your observations by identifying the teacher strategies and child responses in separate columns.

Child Behavior/Comments	Teacher Response

READ AND REFLECT 8

Name: _____

Before coming to workshop 8: "Deepening Children's Science Understandings," read about the teacher's role in "Resources" (p. 73) and excerpts from a teacher's journal (p. 10), both in the teacher's guide. Respond to these questions as you reflect on what you read.

1. In what ways did the teacher in the excerpts from a teacher's journal encourage the children's exploration? What strategies did she use? Note exactly what she did and the date of the entry.

2. In what ways did the teacher deepen children's science understanding? What strategies did she use? Note exactly what she did and the date of the entry.

3. In what ways did the teacher promote early math and literacy learning? What strategies did she use? Note exactly what she did and the date of the entry.

Using Books to Extend Science Learning

AT A GLANCE

Purpose:
- Learn how to select books and use them to enrich children's exploration of buildings
- Learn how to use books that stimulate science inquiry and learning

Activity	Time	Materials
Examine use of books to enrich the children's exploration of structures Guide teachers as they examine different categories of books and consider the varied ways books can enrich children's investigations.	25 minutes	• Chart: "Strategies for the Use of Books"
Provide overview of how to use books Review the types of books that might be used in an exploration of structures, the role of books in science and literacy learning, and ways for using books in the building centers.	25 minutes	• Overhead projector, screen, and overheads 9.1–9.3
Evaluate use of books about structures Guide teachers as they evaluate selected books for classroom use and plan for the use of one book.	45 minutes	• Sample books • Copies of "Small Group Discussion about Books"

Preassignment: Have teachers bring books they have been using that are related to structures. Read the sections on extensions and books and media in the teacher's guide (see p. 70).

Advanced Workshop 9:
Using Books to Extend Science Learning

OBJECTIVES

- Learn how to select books and use them to enrich children's exploration of buildings

- Learn how to use books to stimulate science inquiry and learning

OVERVIEW

- Examine use of books to enrich children's exploration of structures (25 minutes)

- Provide overview of how to use books (20 minutes)

- Evaluate use of books about structures (45 minutes)

INSTRUCTOR PREPARATION

- **GIVE ASSIGNMENT TO TEACHERS.** At least a week before the workshop, tell teachers you want them to read the sections on extensions and books and media in the teacher's guide, and to bring a few (three to five) books they have been using in their structures exploration.

- **COLLECT BOOKS IN EACH OF THE CATEGORIES.** To ensure having a variety of books available, collect some on your own.

MATERIALS

- Three to four books from each of the following categories: (Note: See pp. 82–87 of the teacher's guide for a list of recommended books within each category.)

    - Nonfiction: informational books, image books, and biographies

    - Fiction: fact and fantasy, real-life fiction

    - Poetry books

- Copies of "Small Group Discussion about Books"

- Chart: "Strategies for the Use of Books" with two columns: "Book Title" and "Strategies for Use"

Activity

EXAMINE USE OF BOOKS TO ENRICH CHILDREN'S EXPLORATION (25 MINUTES)

PURPOSE: This interactive activity will acknowledge the teachers' current work and encourage collaboration that might be extended outside the workshop setting.

1. **INTRODUCE THE WORKSHOP** (5 minutes). Begin the workshop by mentioning the importance of books—their value to literacy development as well as science learning. Provide an overview of the content of this workshop. Confirm that the teachers have brought some books with them.

2. **ASK PARTICIPANTS TO SHARE BOOKS THEY HAVE USED AS PART OF THEIR EXPLORATION OF STRUCTURES** (20 minutes). Focus the discussion on how teachers chose these books, what they hoped the children would gain, and how teachers have used them. Allow enough time for teachers to share one of their books and how they are using it. Ask for specifics with questions such as the following:

   - When did you introduce this book in the exploration and why?

   - How did you use this book with children? What did you accomplish?

   - How did the children respond?

   Write titles and their uses on the prepared chart. Look for uses such as the following:

   - Children wanted to build buildings like those pictured in the book.

   - This book encouraged children to take on the challenge of building bridges.

   - This book introduced the work of architects and children are doing more representations of their buildings.

OVERVIEW OF HOW TO USE BOOKS (20 MINUTES)

PURPOSE: Help teachers understand the role books can play in learning and the different kinds of books that are important for use.

Show overheads to begin. As you show them, provide examples of books that relate to the points you are making.

OVERHEAD 9.1: SCIENCE BOOKS AND SCIENCE LEARNING

- **Stimulate science inquiry and thinking**
  Books can provide new challenges to children—How can you make your house as strong as the third little pig? Can you build a castle like this one? They can also stimulate analytical thinking—How is this skyscraper similar to John's? How are they different? I wonder how we could make windows like these in our buildings?

- **Provide images and examples of careers in science**
  Books provide children with examples of careers in which science knowledge is important, such as an engineer, architect, or construction worker.

- **Provide information and ideas relevant to children's scientific inquiries**
  If we look closely at these pictures, can we figure out how to use bricks to make a strong wall? This is what a pyramid looks like. Do you want to use this picture as you make yours?

- **Connect science exploration with the world outside the classroom**
  Most books that reflect images or text about building will help children make connections to the outside world.

OVERHEAD 9.2: SCIENCE BOOKS AND LITERACY DEVELOPMENT

- **Build language skills**
  Books introduce children to new vocabulary and contribute to conceptual understandings. They stimulate children's use of language as they question, explain, and retell the stories.

- **Introduce many genres of books about science**
  Use of varied genre expands children's understanding of books, the kinds of language used in books, and various uses of books. At this point you might review the kinds of fiction, nonfiction, and poetry books that are talked about in the teacher's guide or show examples. Be sure everyone understands these distinctions.

- **Engage children with print**
  Books are one of the many experiences we want children to have that will contribute to their growing understanding of print. At first many children think that the pictures convey the story. An important learning goal for the preschool years is building the understanding that print also conveys a message and that print is made up of letters and words.

- **Develop a love of books**
  The connection of books to a science topic that is interesting to the children contributes to their love of books and their desire to use books in varied ways.

OVERHEAD 9.3: USES OF BOOKS ABOUT BUILDING

- **As references when building**
  Display books in the block area so that they are easily accessible while children are working. Have books that show different kinds of buildings and how they are made. Encourage reference to them.

- **To read aloud and discuss**
  Facilitate conversations in which children discuss ideas presented in books, compare ideas or images from several sources (such as books, posters, or their own buildings), and critically analyze the feasibility of ideas presented in books.

- **To read aloud as an introduction to a new idea or challenge**
  Books can be used to introduce a new idea such as how to lay bricks or a challenge such as building a house as strong as the third pig's, or making a castle tower for Rapunzel.

- **To look at and talk about**
  Many books that you will find to stimulate children's building investigations will not be appropriate for reading aloud. Often this will be because they have great pictures but the text is not appropriate or interesting. But sitting with a child or small group of children and looking at the pictures and talking about them is a great activity. It will lead children to some new insights about their work, and stimulate them to try new kinds of buildings or new building strategies.

EVALUATE USE OF BOOKS ABOUT STRUCTURES (45 MINUTES)

PURPOSE: Help teachers identify ways they can use different kinds of books to enrich children's exploration of building.

1. **PROVIDE INSTRUCTIONS AND TIME FOR THE SMALL GROUP TASK** (20 minutes). Ask participants to form small groups of three or four. Give each group several books, all from the same category (so one group will have information books, another image books, and so on). Also distribute the "Small Group Discussion about Books" handout. Ask groups to look through their books and use the questions on the handout to discuss how they might

use this type of book with children. Finally, they should make a plan for one book in particular. Mention that one person in each group should serve as a recorder. Allow twenty minutes for this small group activity.

2. **FACILITATE GROUP REPORTS** (25 minutes). The amount of time depends somewhat on how many groups you have. Try to structure the time so each group has time to give a report.

Bring the whole group together. Ask one person from each group to share key points that were raised during their small group discussions and a few ideas about how they would use one of the books.

You may want to highlight the following points during the whole group debriefing:

- There are different types of books that teachers can use with children to extend their exploration of building. Some of these books, such as picture books, are usually read cover to cover. In contrast, children may only look at select pages of information books, carefully observing images or finding needed information.

- Teachers sometimes have difficulty finding a place for fiction in a building exploration. Suggest they use familiar stories to deepen children's understanding of a scientific idea. For example, a story such as "The Three Little Pigs" can be used to stimulate a discussion about building materials and design. "Rapunzel" and "The Three Billy Goats Gruff" might be used to interest children in castles, towers, and bridges. The David Macaulay books, such as *Pyramid* and *Castle*, offer a unique view of structures with drawings of the building process.

- Teachers can make a special effort to display books that have engaging pictures related to structures.

- Books can be connected to children's experiences in and out of the classroom. While on a walk, the children may see a bridge and in a follow-up discussion a book can be used to introduce a variety of bridges or give a picture of how a bridge is built. A book can be used to introduce different kinds of houses or to focus the children on different features of houses such as walls, windows, and staircases.

Conclude by reviewing the different categories of books that appear on pp. 70–72 of the teacher's guide. Suggest that teachers use the list of recommended books, choosing from each of the categories to enrich their exploration. Let them know when and where the next training activity will be.

Suggested Next Steps

- If you want to further pursue the ways that inquiry-based science promotes literacy development, you might offer the representation workshops.

- Plan guided discussions that provide an opportunity for teachers to further share their experiences with books.

- Conduct observations of teachers when they are using books. Have a follow-up conference, helping teachers examine their practice.

- Suggest readings from the following references:

  Learning to Read and Write: Developmentally Appropriate Practices for Young Children, by the National Association for the Education of Young Children (NAEYC, 1998)

  Taking Inquiry Outdoors: Reading, Writing, and Science Beyond the Classroom Walls, by Barbara Bourne (Stenhouse, 2000)

SMALL GROUP DISCUSSION ABOUT BOOKS

Use these questions to guide your small group discussion.

1. What are the special features of this type of book (for example: provides accurate information, photos offer realistic images, illustrations are beautiful, and so on)?

2. When would you use this type of book with children?

3. How might you use this type of book to enrich children's explorations of buildings?

4. What do you think are some of the benefits of using this type of book with children (namely, what can children gain)?

5. Is this book scientifically accurate? If not, how would you deal with that?

Assessing Children's Science Learning

AT A GLANCE

Purpose:
- Become familiar with the assessment tools in the teacher's guide
- Practice using the observation records and plan for their systematic use

Activity	Time	Materials
Provide overview of assessment tools in the teacher's guide Offer a framework for assessing children's science learning—its purpose and the process	15 minutes	• Overhead projector, screen, and overhead 10.1
Conduct observation of young naturalists at work Use the observation record form to assess children's science learning	45 minutes	• Chart: "Observing Young Builders" • VCR, monitor, and video vignette 3: "Open Exploration of Unit Blocks" • Copies of observation record
Relate to teachers' practices Discuss ways teachers can systematically use the observation record and the learning record to regularly assess children's inquiry skills and science understandings.	30 minutes	

Preassignment: Read the "Observation and Assessment" section in the teacher's guide (see p. 77). Use the observation record in the teacher's guide to document what children say and do during a building exploration.

Advanced Workshop 10:
Assessing Children's Science Learning

OBJECTIVES

- Become familiar with the assessment tools in the teacher's guide
- Practice using the observation records and plan for their systematic use

OVERVIEW

- Overview of assessment tools in the teacher's guide (15 minutes)
- Practice observing young builders at work (45 minutes)
- Relate assessment practices to own teaching practice (30 minutes)

INSTRUCTOR PREPARATION

- **REVIEW VIGNETTE 3: "OPEN EXPLORATION OF UNIT BLOCKS."** View it and note the aspects that you will highlight during the workshop. This vignette is also used in workshop 3.

MATERIALS

- Chart: "Observing Young Builders"
- VCR, monitor, and video cued to vignette 3: "Open Exploration of Unit Blocks"
- Overhead projector, screen, and overhead 10.1
- Copies of transcript for vignette 3 and an observation record for each teacher

Activity

OVERVIEW OF ASSESSMENT IN SCIENCE EXPLORATIONS (15 MINUTES)

PURPOSE: This activity will set the stage for those that follow by providing an assessment framework for science learning, its purpose and process.

1. **INTRODUCE THE WORKSHOP AND DISCUSS THE PURPOSE OF ASSESSMENT** (5 minutes). Give an overview of the activities. Ask teachers why they think assessment is important and what it involves. Allow them to share their ideas, reinforcing those that refer to assessment as a way to make informed decisions about teaching and learning. Emphasize these points:

   - Assessment provides information about children's interests, abilities, and understandings.
   - Ultimately, the teacher learns about the effectiveness of her teaching through assessment.
   - Assessment is ongoing and the process includes documentation, reflection, and planning.

2. INTRODUCE THE KEY ELEMENTS OF THE ASSESSMENT PROCESS USING OVERHEAD 10.1 (5 minutes).

OVERHEAD 10.1: KEY ELEMENTS OF ASSESSMENT PROCESS

- **Collecting data**
  You might want to ask teachers what they think data means in this context. Emphasize the value of regularly collecting multiple sources of data (written observations, photographs, video- and audiotape, or samples of children's work) that can provide insights about children's inquiry skills and their understandings of the science concepts. Suggest that teachers document at least one observation per child every two weeks, and collect one work sample per child per week.

- **Analyzing data regularly**
  This data will only have meaning when teachers take time to think about it. Teachers should examine varied documents to gauge each child's engagement and science learning. At the same time, teachers should look at the class as a whole and how it is going.

- **Drawing conclusions and making decisions**
  Conclusions are about the important links between teaching and learning. Are your children engaged? Are they deepening their understanding of the science concepts by using inquiry? Are all children making progress? What does this mean for your teaching? These are the key questions that will lead to conclusions and making informed decisions about next steps.

---

3. ASK TEACHERS TO OPEN THEIR TEACHER'S GUIDES TO "SCIENCE OUTCOMES: SCIENCE IN-QUIRY SKILLS AND SCIENCE CONCEPTS" (5 minutes) in the appendices (pp. 97–98). Review the chart with them, pointing out the kinds of information it provides. Explain that they will use this chart as a basis for assessing children's science learning.

PRACTICE USING THE OBSERVATION RECORD (45 MINUTES)

PURPOSE: This activity will help teachers learn what to look for as they observe and document children's work using the observation record form. Such an activity will help teachers focus on science concepts and inquiry skills as they assess children's learning.

1. OBSERVE AND DISCUSS VIGNETTE 3: "OPEN EXPLORATION OF UNIT BLOCKS" (45 minutes).

   a. Start by asking the teachers what they look for as they assess their children's engagement and understandings. Note their ideas on the chart, "Observing Young Builders." Add important ideas that they do not mention.

   > Look for ideas such as whether or not the children are showing interest and staying with an activity, the aspects of inquiry they are using, the ways they are communicating ideas, the ideas they have, the science concepts they are exploring, and the quality of their interaction with other children.

   b. Introduce vignette 3 by saying that this vignette was filmed in a Boston Head Start classroom. They will observe a group of five children who are building in the block area. James, Victor, and Armin are working together. Thalia and Roney are working on their own. Roney's building is not shown. Four of these children are English language learners. Their first languages are Farsi, Arabic, Albanian, and Spanish. Tell teachers they will be watching the vignette twice; the second time they will take notes.

c. Show the vignette. Then ask teachers what they noticed about the children's engagement and their understandings. Listen to their comments, asking for specifics and keeping teachers focused on what they actually saw, not their interpretation of it. Highlight any differences of opinion or questions.

d. Prepare for the next viewing by passing out the observation record and transcript. Remind them that their notes should be objective—not interpretations. Also encourage them to use the outcomes chart to focus their observations.

e. Show the vignette again. Then ask teachers what they noticed this time. During the conversation, highlight important aspects of documenting observations:

- Document—Complete and objective notes are critical. Have some teachers tell the class what they wrote. You might want to take one small sequence and get a couple of variations, working toward a more complete statement. (Mention that this is similar to one major goal for the children—to observe and describe what they see.)

- Analyze—Consider the variations in children's engagement and understandings that come when you begin to interpret the observation notes. Reflecting on what children say and do provides insights into their level of engagement and their science understandings. In this vignette, all five children are productively engaged in building. The two buildings show some understanding of how the children are balancing blocks and creating a building that is stable: they are tall, built from a block foundation, and not on the rug. They have different design features that provide balance and stability. One uses two columns and some bracing; the other depends on careful placement of the blocks. There is still some trial and error; for example, the attempt to balance a block on the props and the effort to get the arch on the building (near the end of the vignette). This particular sequence showed good cooperation as Armin and James worked together to find the right side for balancing the block on their tower.

- Plan—Observations can help teachers plan next steps. For example, seeing what each child has done to create stability can help a teacher prepare for some recording of data and discussion of the children's ideas.

DISCUSS OWN CLASSROOM OBSERVATIONS (30 MINUTES)

PURPOSE: This is an opportunity for the teachers to connect their new understandings about assessment to their own classroom practice. They can also look for ways to incorporate the assessment tools into their ongoing work.

1. CONDUCT AN INFORMAL CONVERSATION (20 minutes). Ask teachers how they have connected this approach to their own assessment practices. Use the following questions to focus their comments: (Continue to refer to the outcomes chart.)

- What kind of science engagement do you see in your classrooms? Let teachers talk about what they are seeing for a few minutes. Then ask them to examine the science concepts (noted on the outcomes chart) being explored and the inquiry their children are engaged in.

- In what ways have you recorded your observations? For instance, teachers may place clipboards around the room with copies of the observation form so they are always available. Also, encourage use of multimedia, including audio and tape recording, because such methods capture moments that allow for deeper reflection. Elicit issues teachers have with the process and encourage them to help each other resolve barriers they encounter. For example, talk about how they might use the observation records regularly.

- Are you systematically analyzing your data? Find out when they are finding time for reflection, letting them learn from each other. Allow issues to surface and help teachers find solutions. Be sure they understand that observations and other documents becomes more valuable if they are used for assessment purposes, informing teaching on a regular basis.

2. **INTRODUCE THE OBSERVATION RECORD** (10 minutes) by asking them to turn to p. 93 in their teacher's guides. Explain that this is a way of recording science inquiry and understandings over the period of one exploration. Mention that the outcomes will help them with the meaning of some of these items. Use Victor as an example and ask what might be noted about him based on this one observation. While you cannot distinguish "sometimes" and "consistently," you can identify things that he reveals about his understandings and inquiry skills. Look for ideas such as doesn't have a word for triangle, or knows not to add to others' buildings without asking.

Conclude by sharing the topic of the next workshop and when it is scheduled. Give teachers any assignment you want them to complete in preparation.

Suggested Next Steps

- Follow up with individual teachers to see if they are finding ways to use the assessment tools in their classrooms. Key to their success with the tools is their ability to make sense of the science in the children's explorations. Look for any issues they might have with the science and provide support when needed. One strategy is to observe them and talk about the science. Another would be to view vignettes and just talk about the science understandings evident in each one.

- The representation and documentation panel workshops all reinforce ideas about assessment.

- Use upcoming guided discussions to examine and discuss what children's work samples and conversations reveal about their level of engagement, inquiry skills, and science understandings.

- Suggest readings from the following references:

  "The Role of the Constructivist Teacher," chapter 4 in *The Young Child as Scientist: A Constructivist Approach to Early Childhood Science Education*, by C. Chaille and L. Britain (Allyn & Bacon, 2003)

  Learning in Science: The Implications of Children's Science, by R. Osborne and P. Freyberg (Heinemann, 1985)

Encouraging Representation

AT A GLANCE

Purpose:

- Gain an understanding of the purpose of observational drawing and other forms of representation in young children's science learning
- Identify strategies for encouraging representation
- Practice assessing children's representations
- Learn to select and display appropriate materials

Activity	Time	Materials
Provide an overview of the role of representation in inquiry science Use overheads to introduce this session and discuss how representation can promote children's science learning.	15 minutes	• Overhead projector, screen, and overheads 11.1 and 11.2
Discuss encouraging representation through conversation Use a video vignette to discuss the ways a teacher can support representation.	30 minutes	• VCR, monitor, and video cued to vignette 6: "Encouraging Representation" • Chart: "Strategies for Encouraging Representation" • Copies of vignette observation form and transcript of vignette 6
Discuss encouraging representation through the environment and routines Facilitate a conversation about appropriate representation materials and how to make them accessible to the children during their exploration. Share the importance of regular routines.	15 minutes	
Help teachers assess children's representations Guide teachers as they analyze overheads of children's work, using the document annotation form from the teacher's guide.	30 minutes	• Overheads 11.3–11.7 • Copies of document annotations

Postassignment: Review the section on representation in "The Teacher's Role," which appears on p. 75 of the teacher's guide.

Advanced Workshop 11: Encouraging Representation

OBJECTIVES

- Gain an understanding of the purpose of observational drawing and other forms of representation in young children's science learning
- Identify strategies for encouraging representation
- Practice assessing children's representations
- Learn to select and display appropriate materials

OVERVIEW

- Provide overview of the role of representation in inquiry science (15 minutes)
- Discuss encouraging representation through conversation (30 minutes)
- Discuss encouraging representation through the environment and routines (15 minutes)
- Help teachers assess children's representations (30 minutes)

INSTRUCTOR PREPARATION

- **GIVE ASSIGNMENT.** At least one week before the workshop ask teachers to review the section on representation that appears in "Resources" on p. 77 of the teacher's guide.
- **REVIEW VIGNETTE.** View the vignette and note teaching strategies that you will highlight in the workshop.

MATERIALS

- Copies of document annotations (p. 94 in the teacher's guide)
- Overhead projector, screen, and overheads 11.1–11.7
- VCR, monitor, and video cued to vignette 6: "Encouraging Representation"
- Chart: "Strategies for Encouraging Representation"
- Copies of vignette observation form and transcript of vignette 6 for each teacher

Activity

OVERVIEW OF THE ROLE OF REPRESENTATION (15 MINUTES)

PURPOSE: Understanding how representation can promote children's inquiry and science understandings will be key to the teacher's work with children. This overview will also set the stage for the rest of this workshop.

1. **INTRODUCE THE WORKSHOP AND PROVIDE AN OVERVIEW** of the purpose of representation in science teaching and learning (5 minutes). Provide an overview of the activities in this workshop. Show overhead 11.1. Note that Pablo has drawn a picture of his block building.

His work shows what happens when children do representational drawing regularly. Use the following discussion points to talk about the purpose of representation:

- Encourages children to look closely at their buildings, their parts and shapes, and spacing of the blocks.

- Builds abilities to use multiple media to communicate observations and ideas.

- Encourages new questions.

- Promotes early literacy.

- Is a form of data collection used regularly by architects, engineers, and scientists. For example, blueprints and models are used for planning, reflection, and analysis.

2. **TALK ABOUT YOUNG CHILDREN AND REPRESENTATION FOR A FEW MINUTES** (10 minutes). Show overhead 11.2 (a more primitive drawing) and make the following points:

- Three- and four-year-olds are just learning to draw. Their motor abilities are not fully developed and they are just learning about symbolic representation.

- Children's early representations often focus on the overall shape of a building. Refer to overhead 11.2 as an example. Over time, children's awareness of the parts that make up the whole becomes evident in drawings that represent not just shape, but also different parts (such as the blocks in Pablo's tower). Fine-tip drawing tools are needed to capture these details.

- Emphasize that children need tools and plenty of time to practice. Clipboards in the block area are very useful for making representation easy to access and do.

- Each child will have their own preference for the medium in which they choose to communicate. In part, this is developmental—can they grasp a big marker or pen? It may also be a difference in style. Some children prefer three-dimensional representation, such as clay or collage, and others prefer movement.

ENCOURAGING REPRESENTATION THROUGH CONVERSATION (30 MINUTES)

PURPOSE: Teachers will generate a list of strategies they can use to encourage representation in their own classrooms.

1. **DISCUSS THE READING ASSIGNMENT** (10 minutes). Ask, "What are some important points about encouraging representation mentioned in the teacher's guide?" List these ideas on the chart you prepared. Encourage teachers to think about how different parts of the guide (such as the teacher's role, open exploration, and focused exploration) support their work with children around representation.

2. **INTRODUCE AND SHOW VIGNETTE 6** (20 minutes). Start by saying that this vignette was filmed in a Head Start program. It shows a teacher and two children working at a table, building and drawing. Distribute the vignette observation form and transcript, and ask teachers to note strategies the teacher in the video uses to encourage representation and engage children with science.

   Show the vignette and ask teachers what they noticed. Note their strategies on the chart you prepared. Ask how these strategies promote science learning.

Look for ideas like these:

- Asks children to represent, provides materials, and gives simple instructions
- Shows value for their work through her presence and encouragement
- Focuses children on details by using descriptive language and words such as *rectangle* and *triangle,* and calls attention to details such as height
- Encourages labeling with names, provides cards

ENCOURAGING REPRESENTATION— THE ENVIRONMENT AND ROUTINES (15 MINUTES)

PURPOSE: An important part of encouraging representation is the choice of materials and their accessibility, as well as regular routines. This conversation will highlight key strategies.

1. **TALK ABOUT THE SELECTION OF MATERIALS FOR A FEW MINUTES** (5 minutes). Ask teachers how the selection of materials can encourage representation. Note their strategies on the chart, seeing that the following points are made:

   - Materials must be selected that allow for accurate representation of the object's characteristics. For example, drawing is a medium that allows for representation of many characteristics but only two dimensions. The amount of detail possible varies with the type of pen or marker being used. Fine-tip markers allow for more detail. Wire is a medium that is excellent for re-creating shape but might not be good for capturing all of the details. Mention that their expectations should be in line with the medium's potential.

   - Varied materials should be available. Consider both two- and three-dimensional material as important. A collage, using recycled materials of various shapes, can be an important stimulus for careful examination of a structure. In addition, constructing with collage materials provides new challenges with the science concepts. Two-dimensional collage can also be created using paper cut in the shapes of the blocks. This is an excellent way to get children to focus on the elements of their building if they have been representing the overall shape.

   - A visit from an expert (such as an architect with sketches) can help children think about drawing as a part of planning a building. It also gives them a different perspective to consider as they draw.

2. **TALK ABOUT THE IMPORTANCE OF ACCESSIBILITY** (2 to 3 minutes). Ask teachers how to display materials so they inspire representation. Be sure to make the following points:

   - Children should be able to get materials and put them back without help.
   - Materials should be available in or next to the places where they are building.
   - Clipboards are especially useful for drawing in the block area.
   - Representation should be done when the building is in view.
   - Photos of structures might be used when making three-dimensional representations when it is difficult to have the original structure present.

3. **TALK ABOUT THE IMPORTANCE OF REGULAR ROUTINES** (5 minutes). Ask teachers how regular routines support children's representation. Note their strategies on the chart and be sure to make the following points:

   - Regular encouragement from the teacher, with reminders or suggestions, can help children make representation a part of their routine. Give a few examples such as, "I see your building is done. Would you like to draw a picture of it while it is still standing?" or "I have some new collage materials. Would you like to try re-creating your building with them?"

   - Large group time is a good time to show that you value children's work by sharing it.

4. **FINALLY, TALK ABOUT DISPLAYING CHILDREN'S WORK** (2 to 3 minutes). Make these points about things teachers should consider as they display children's work:

   - Displaying children's work shows that you value what they do.

   - Displays allow children to revisit their work and build on their ideas.

   - Displays should be at the children's eye level.

   - Displays should reflect children's current interests and investigations.

   - Displays can be a powerful way to educate parents about the important learning that is going on in the classroom.

HELP TEACHERS ASSESS CHILDREN'S REPRESENTATIONS (30 MINUTES)

PURPOSE: This activity will help teachers understand how children represent buildings. By carefully reflecting on and assessing children's representations, teachers can learn about children's inquiry skills and their science understanding.

1. **INTRODUCE THE ACTIVITY** (5 minutes). Tell teachers that they will be looking at some children's work samples and talking about the science understandings being communicated. Ask the teachers to open the teacher's guide to the outcomes chart in the appendices. Explain that they will refer to this chart as they assess children's work. Distribute the document annotations and refer to their placement in the teacher's guide. Make the following points:

   - Note that using the forms will help teachers focus their analysis of each piece of work. These completed forms can also help families appreciate what their children are learning.

   - Representations are best understood in conjunction with a conversation where the children elaborate on the meaning of their own work. The following samples were selected to highlight this point.

2. **SHOW AND DISCUSS OVERHEADS** (25 minutes). Show as many overheads (11.3–11.6) as time allows. Ask teachers to talk about what they see and what they might write on a document annotation.

OVERHEAD 11.3: REBECCA'S BRIDGE

Context: During a building structures exploration, Rebecca has drawn one of her structures.

Science being explored/evidence: She is working with how she can create a span that is anchored and stable.

A good discussion topic for the teacher and Rebecca would be talking about the different parts of the bridge, what perspective they are drawn from, and what the shapes at the bottom represent. This will focus her on the parts of the building and how she sees them. They could also talk about what makes it strong and how these elements are shown.

OVERHEAD 11.4: KATHERINE'S EIFFEL TOWER

Context: Engaged in building exploration and making three-dimensional representations of buildings, Katherine first represented the Eiffel Tower from a picture in a book, then created her three-dimensional collage.

Science being explored/evidence: Katherine has had to be careful where and how she placed her blocks so that her tower would be tall and stable and look a bit like the Eiffel Tower. She did this first with blocks, then faced a whole new set of issues as she worked with the collage materials.

The teacher might talk with Katherine, asking her to describe her experience, why she chose these materials, what was challenging, and how she dealt with difficulties. Using the photo of the Eiffel Tower, she might talk about the parts—what the egg carton in Katherine's building represents, and so on.

OVERHEAD 11.5: CHIDEMMA'S TOWER

Context: As part of a building structures exploration, the class is focused on towers and has taken a field trip to a Boston skyscraper, the John Hancock Tower.

Science being explored/evidence: Chidemma is focused on height and refers to two units of measurement as she compares structures—the height of Oneyda, the assistant teacher, and counting blocks. Her drawing quite accurately reflects both of these.

A conversation with Chidemma might focus on the data she has so carefully represented. The teacher might get her to talk about whether or not the actual towers leaned the way they do in the picture. This conversation could tap what she knows about creating stability in towers.

OVERHEAD 11.6: THREE-DIMENSIONAL COLLAGE

Context: This is also a three-dimensional representation created during an exploration of structures.

Science being explored/evidence: Similar to the Eiffel Tower, this child has worked with very different materials to make a building that will stand up. This has happened twice: once with the building, and again with the three-dimensional representation.

Good conversation questions would be similar to the ones asked above about Katherine's representation of the Eiffel Tower. Ask the child to compare problems encountered when building with blocks and those encountered working with the collage materials.

Show overhead 11.7. Encourage teachers to use this form to annotate photos, work samples, transcripts, or any other documents that they may have. When filling out the form, teachers should highlight what the document reveals about children's building and their understanding of science concepts. Teachers should attach their annotation to each document.

Close by letting the teachers know about the next workshop, as well as the time and location.

Suggested Next Steps

- Make a handout of the strategies and distribute it.

- Follow up with workshop 12, which builds on the content of this workshop.

- Plan guided discussions in which the teachers can share and discuss representations and useful strategies for encouraging representation.

- Conduct observations, helping teachers develop a repertoire of strategies for encouraging representation in their classrooms.

- Suggest readings from the following references:

"A Child Constructs an Understanding of a Water Wheel in Five Media," by George Forman (*Childhood Education,* 1996)

"Negotiating with Art Media to Deepen Learning," by George Forman (*Child Care Information Exchange,* 1996)

Observation Drawing with Children: A Framework for Teachers, by N. R. Smith (Teachers College Press, 1998)

Transcript of Video Vignette 6:
Encouraging Representation

Scene: Three children—Ikechukwu, John Michael, and Roney—are building and drawing during choice time in a Head Start classroom. Ikechukwu and John Michael are working with table blocks and Roney is in the block area.

Teacher: Ikechukwu, look. Remember the other day when you took your picture and you were building with Kapla blocks? You were trying to make it very high. Do you remember? Did you make this one higher *(pointing to structure on table)* or did this one go higher *(pointing to paper)*?

Ikechukwu: *(Points to structure.)*

Teacher: You think this one went higher. I think so too.

Ikechukwu: *(Draws on paper.)*

Teacher: Are you drawing your building now?

(Scene shifts to John Michael building a structure, then back to Ikechukwu and the teacher.)

Ikechukwu: *(Drawing on paper, but looking elsewhere.)*

Teacher: Remember to look at your building on the paper when you are drawing.

(Scene shifts to Roney on floor drawing, then back to John Michael and teacher.)

Teacher: *(To John Michael)* There's a lot of places to climb in your structure—a lot of places for people to climb over and what do they do when they get up to the top?

John Michael: The just see the whole world.

Teacher: Oh, they can sit up there and see the whole world. Why is it they can see so far when they're up there?

John Michael: They can see their houses.

Teacher: They can see their houses. Do they like to sit up there and look all over and see the whole world? Would you like to draw a picture of your structure with the black marker?

John Michael: I don't know how to.

Teacher: Well, see how Ikechukwu does it? He looks at his structure and then he looks at the paper and he starts to draw the way it looks. And then he looks at his structure again and then he looks back at the paper. Do you want to give it a try?

John Michael: *(Nods yes; takes marker and starts to draw.)*

Teacher: *(Off screen.)* Show me this part of your structure. Where's that part?

Teacher: *(To Ikechukwu, pointing to his drawing.)* Tell me about those lines you just made.

Ikechukwu: *(Taps teacher and points to his structure.)*

Teacher: *(Pointing to drawing)* These parts here and this part here going across? I was looking at this one and it goes up, up, up, up, up. It looks like this part *(pointing to structure)*. See it? It goes up so high *(pointing to drawing)*. It looks like that one *(pointing to structure)*.

Ikechukwu: *(Draws line upward on his drawing.)*

Teacher: Oh, you make it higher in your picture. You made it higher. Can you show the blocks?

Ikechukwu: *(Keeps drawing.)*

Teacher: *(Pointing to drawing.)* Wow! You made a big one here. It's a square shape.

Teacher: *(Looking at another child who is off screen.)* You're doing it. See?

Roney: *(Brings drawing to teacher.)* Look at *(inaudible)*.

Teacher: Oh, good. *(Inaudible)* wrote your name on it. I'm glad.

Teacher: Let me come and see John Michael. *(Goes over to John Michael.)* When you were drawing a structure, what did you draw first? Show me what you drew first.

John Michael: I drew this first *(points to drawing)*.

Teacher: Show me with your hand or your finger or the marker.

John Michael: I did that like *(inaudible)*.

Teacher: You did that part first? What part is that on your building?

John Michael: That's one that goes up.

Teacher: That's the part that goes up.

John Michael: The cars *(inaudible)*.

Teacher: And the cars go around on the outside? Like around this way *(circling with her finger)*.

John Michael: Yah.

Teacher: How can you show on your paper how high this is—because this is very high *(pointing to structure)*. Is there some way to show that on your paper?

John Michael: Yah. This is one that goes there. This is one that goes up.

Teacher: That goes up. Can you show me where this part is on your picture? Where's this part? *(Points to top of structure.)* The top where the people sit up on top.

John Michael: This is *(inaudible; showing drawing to teacher)*.

TRANSCRIPT OF VIDEO VIGNETTE 6: ENCOURAGING REPRESENTATION (CONT'D)

Teacher: Okay. So that's where the people sit? You told me that's where the people sit to look out over the world. Do you want to write your name on there?

John Michael: I don't know how to write my name.

Teacher: Do you want to get your name from the writing area or do you just want to try it your own way?

John Michael: Just do it.

Teacher: Just do it your own way?

John Michael: *(Draws on paper.)*

Teacher: *(Off screen)* Ikechukwu, what do you want to do next? Do you want me to take a picture? Do you want me to take a picture with the camera?

ADVANCED WORKSHOP 5: VIGNETTE OBSERVATION FORM

Note your observations by identifying the teacher strategies and child responses in separate columns.

Child Behavior/Comments	Teacher Response

Using Children's Representations as Teaching Tools

AT A GLANCE

Purpose:

- Examine the ways representation can be used to deepen children's science learning
- Have science talks about children's representations

Activity	Time	Materials
Help teachers assess children's representations Working in small groups, help teachers to assess representations from their own classrooms.	30 minutes	• Copies of document annotations
Discuss using representations as teaching tools Use vignettes to help teachers identify strategies for using representations to deepen children's science understandings.	35 minutes	• Chart: "Strategies for Talking about Representations" • VCR, monitor, and video cued to vignette 7: "Talking about Drawings of Buildings" • Overhead projector, screen, and overheads 11.7 and 12.1 • Copies of vignette observation form and transcripts for vignette 7
Help teachers use children's representations to stimulate science talks Support teachers as they plan goals and questions for a conversation with one of the children about their representation.	20 minutes	• Copies of "Representation Conversation Planning Form"

Preassignment: Bring three to five observational drawings or other forms of representation (such as a collage or sculpture) to the workshop.

Advanced Workshop 12: Using Children's Representations as Teaching Tools

OBJECTIVES

- Examine ways representation can be used to deepen children's science learning
- Plan science talks about children's representations

OVERVIEW

- Help teachers assess children's representations (30 minutes)
- Discuss using representations as teaching tools (35 minutes)
- Help teachers use children's representations to plan a science talk (25 minutes)

INSTRUCTOR PREPARATION

- **GIVE ASSIGNMENT.** At least one week before the workshop, ask teachers to collect three to five representations from their class. Suggest diversity, either in children's ability or in the medium used.

- **REVIEW VIGNETTE.** View the vignette, noting aspects you will highlight in the workshop.

> The activities in this workshop assume that teachers have already participated in advanced workshop 11. In workshop 11, they learn to fill out document annotations, and in this workshop they start using them to assess the children's work.

MATERIALS

- Chart: "Strategies for Talking about Representation"
- VCR, monitor, and video cued to vignette 7: "Talking about Drawings of Buildings"
- Overhead projector, screen, and overheads 11.7 and 12.1
- Copies of document annotations, transcript for vignette 7, representation conversation planning form, and vignette observation form for everyone

Activity

HELP TEACHERS ASSESS CHILDREN'S REPRESENTATIONS (30 MINUTES)

PURPOSE: This activity will help teachers apply what they are learning as they assess what children's representations reveal about their science understandings.

1. **INTRODUCE THE WORKSHOP AND FIRST TASK** (5 minutes). Provide an overview of the workshop activities. Then show overhead 11.7—the sample document annotation—and review how to fill one out. Pass out two forms to everyone and ask them to select two of the samples they brought that show distinctly different medium or skill levels. Suggest they refer to

the outcomes chart in the resources section of the teacher's guide to complete a document annotation for each of the two samples they have selected. Ask them to form questions on another piece of paper. Tell teachers they have twenty minutes to complete this task.

2. **SUPPORT TEACHERS AS THEY COMPLETE THE DOCUMENT ANNOTATION FORMS** (20 minutes). Go around the room and check on individuals. Help them think through what they want to write when they seem stuck. As they complete their forms, ask them to partner with another teacher who is done. Their partners might have additional thoughts as they examine children's representations.

3. **ASK TEACHERS TO SHARE THEIR THOUGHTS ABOUT THIS EXPERIENCE** (5 minutes). Listen to comments and provide support as teachers think through issues. Teachers might say it was easier to assess representation if they had discussions with children about their work. Emphasize how conversations with children can provide added insights into their work, what they are trying to accomplish, and their science understandings.

USING REPRESENTATIONS AS TEACHING TOOLS (35 MINUTES)

PURPOSE: Talking to children about their representations can help teachers assess children's understandings. Such conversations also provide a teaching opportunity, helping children to reflect on their experiences and their ideas. This activity will help teachers develop a list of strategies for their use.

1. **DISCUSS THE VARIED WAYS REPRESENTATIONS CAN SERVE AS TEACHING TOOLS** (15 minutes). Show overhead 12.1. Point out the term *documentation*, which includes photographs, data charts, dictations, and children's representations.

OVERHEAD 12.1: USE REPRESENTATIONS TO DEEPEN LEARNING AND PROMOTE INQUIRY

- **Build ability to communicate observations and ideas**
  As children talk about their work, encourage them to describe what they have represented. Model using descriptive language yourself.

- **Focus on particular science ideas**
  For example, talk about the parts of the structure and how they have been represented. You might examine the structure (or a photo of it) and the child's representation at the same time.

- **Build a culture of inquiry and collaboration**
  Look at children's work with groups of children. Compare and contrast structures by highlighting the different ways they have been represented. Perspectives, ways of representing blocks, ways of representing height—all are kinds of representation you might find.

- **Connect children's explorations from one day to the next**
  Use their work to call attention to what they were doing a day or two ago. This will help them continue an investigation, moving forward with their inquiry.

- **Recap what has been learned at key points in an exploration**
  Use selections of several children's work to review what they have done and learned before moving on.

- **Stimulate discussion in which children synthesize and analyze their work**
  Use documents to compare, contrast, and draw conclusions about structures they have been building and questions they have been exploring.

Transition to the next activity by saying that they will get a chance to apply these ideas as they look at a video vignette.

2. **View and discuss vignette 7: "Talking about Drawings of Buildings"** (20 minutes). Introduce the vignette by saying that this is Cindy, a teacher from an earlier vignette, and two children, Thalia and Roney, who are both English language learners. Both children are working in the block area. They have been building and are now drawing their structures. Distribute the vignette observation form. Tell teachers that as they view the vignette, they should note the strategies being used next to the appropriate box.

Show the vignette. After viewing, ask teachers to identify strategies (and list on prepared chart) the teacher is using and then talk about other ways these drawings might be used. Every representation does not have a use for each learning goal so you don't need to fill in every box.

During the discussion, emphasize how teachers can use representations to deepen children's science understanding and promote inquiry. Look for ideas like these:

- Build ability to communicate observations and ideas—This was a primary goal of this conversation. Cindy is helping Thalia and Roney use and learn words for relative size, shape, and location (such as long, straight, cylinder, on top), and parts of their structures (such as floor, roof, wall).

- Focus on particular science ideas—This conversation is focused on developing children's understanding of the relationship between their drawings and structures. These talks focus the children on their selection of blocks for different parts of their buildings, design features (such as use of the triangle or the long straight blocks), and how they represent their work. Thalia is encouraged to collect some data when she counts the cylinder blocks.

Some other suggestions include the following:

- Showing the drawing to Thalia the next day or later in the week so she remembers her interest in building high. Roney might be encouraged to make a door or to work on walls. They might also be encouraged to try three-dimensional representations.

- Comparing Thalia and Roney's representation with other children's work and talking about the characteristics of each; highlighting the varied approaches to roofs, walls, and doors; and contrasting the ways they are represented on paper. For example, one child might draw every block in her structure while another creates one shape to represent each part of his building.

Planning a Conversation about Children's Representations (20 minutes)

Purpose: This activity will help the teachers apply to their own classroom what they are learning about using representations as teaching tools.

1. **Set up this planning task** (5 minutes) by distributing the representation conversation planning form. Tell teachers that you are going to give them a chance to use one of their representations to guide a conversation that furthers children's science learning and promotes inquiry. Review the form and answer any questions they have.

2. **Give them ten minutes to work.** Wander around the room and help those who seem to be struggling. Encourage teachers to talk to each other as they work.

3. **BRING THEM TOGETHER TO SHARE IDEAS** (5 minutes). Allow a few minutes for a few of them to share ideas and solve any issues that arise. Encourage them to follow through and have this conversation. Make a point of telling teachers that while this workshop is focused on using children's representations, all forms of documentation can be used as teaching tools in this same way. This would include photographs and records of data.

In conclusion, tell them about the next workshop, when and where it takes place, and which assignments they should complete.

Suggested Next Steps

• Make a handout of the strategies list and distribute it.

• You might follow up with a workshop about making documentation panels.

• Conduct guided discussions in which teachers bring documentation (video- or audiotape) of conversations about children's representations, and analyze them together.

• Observe and have a conference with teachers around a representation conversation.

• Suggest readings from these references:

"Negotiating with Art Media to Deepen Learning," by George Forman (*Child Care Information Exchange*, 1996)

Helping Children Ask Good Questions, by George Forman (Exchange Press, 1996)

TRANSCRIPT OF VIDEO VIGNETTE 7:
TALKING ABOUT DRAWINGS OF BUILDINGS

Scene: Two children—Roney and Thalia—are talking about their drawings of buildings with their teacher.

(Thalia and Roney drawing on paper attached to clipboard.)

Roney: I finish.

Teacher: Do you want to look at your picture together? I'll come over there though. I'll come over there. Because I don't want to—excuse me, Victor. I'm going to just step around you. Don't want anything to fall down. Can we look at your picture together?

Roney: Yes.

Teacher: Oops. Tell me about these blocks. Which ones were you making when you made those long straight ones? Is that those long straight ones? *(Points to structure.)*

Roney: Yes.

Teacher: Is this the floor still?

Roney: Yeah.

Teacher: It is? Tell me about that.

Roney: A house.

Teacher: That's the house. Is it the wall or is it the roof?

Roney: The roof.

Teacher: It's the roof?

Roney: And that's the house. I didn't make the door.

Teacher: You didn't make the door?

Roney: No.

Teacher: Show me the roof on your paper. Up on the top.

Roney: *(Points to drawing)* Yeah.

Teacher: Okay, cool.

Roney: Up on the top.

Teacher: Up on the top. Can we look at that?

Roney: Yes.

Teacher: You're getting all ready. Wow. You know what? I can almost . . . Can I guess what this part is?

Thalia: Yeah.

Teacher: Can I guess that that's your—do you want me to guess or do you want to tell me about it?

Thalia: That's the door.

Teacher: *(Points back and forth from drawing to structure)* That's your door. And you know what? I can tell because you made this shape so carefully—it goes in here just like your door goes in here. See that part—is that the right—is that the same one that I'm looking at? I'll be right with you, thank you. And what about this? Is this the inside part that opens?

Thalia: Right here.

Teacher: Oh, okay. These—1, 2, 3, 4—are these 1, 2, 3, 4? Is that what this is? Now show me on here.

Thalia: *(Points to structure)* 1, 2, 3, 4.

Teacher: Wow, I can sure tell. And what about this part here?

Thalia: That's . . . *(Points to structure)*

Teacher: That's that little tower over there. And is this . . . *(Roney's structure falls.)* Oh, too bad. Oh, honey, you got mad and something knocked over Thalia's. I'm glad nobody got hurt. Thalia, you should really have a hat on. Victor, you should really have a hat on too. I'm trying to be pretty stern about the hats. Thalia, just tell me this part. This triangle that I see here. *(Thalia points to her structure.)* Is that the—oh, that's what I thought. That is so cool. Do you want to put your name on it or do you want me to?

ADVANCED WORKSHOP 12: VIGNETTE OBSERVATION FORM

Goal of Strategy	Strategies in Vignette 7
Build capacity to communicate observations and ideas	
Focus on particular science ideas	
Build a culture of inquiry and collaboration	
Connect children's explorations from one day to the next	
Recap what has been learned	
Help children synthesize and analyze their work	

ADVANCED WORKSHOP 12:
REPRESENTATION CONVERSATION PLANNING FORM

Name: _____

Child: _____

Goal(s) of conversation: _____

_____

_____

Science content to explore : _____

List a few questions that you can use to get the conversation going, and search for deeper meanings along the way. Note the part of the representation that each question might be focused on—for example, you might want to talk about the shape of certain blocks or the particular materials selected for a collage.

Facilitating Science Talks

AT A GLANCE

Purpose:

- Build an understanding of group conversations and the role they play in children's science learning
- Build various strategies for facilitating science talks
- Build an awareness of what inhibits conversations

Activity	Time	Materials
Provide an overview of science talks Let teachers share their early attempts at science talks, the successes and issues. Begin to talk about effective and ineffective strategies.	30 minutes	• Charts: "Strategies for Science Talks" and "Issues We Are Having with Science Talks" • Overhead projector, screen, and overheads 13.1–13.3
Help teachers analyze a small group science talk Use a vignette to highlight the importance of science talks and identify strategies teachers can use to facilitate them.	25 minutes	• VCR, monitor, and video cued to vignette 8: "Constructing a Wall" • Copies of handouts: vignette observation form and transcript of vignette 8
Help teachers analyze a large group science talk Use a transcript to highlight the importance of large group science talks and identify strategies teachers can use to facilitate them.	35 minutes	• VCR, monitor, and video cued to vignette 9: "Group Sharing" • Copies of transcript of vignette 9 and "Strategies for Facilitating Science Talks"

Preassignment: Participants will be asked to pay attention as they talk with children, noting where they are successfully engaging them in thinking about science and where they are having difficulty. They should also complete "Read and Reflect 13."

Advanced Workshop 13: Facilitating Science Talks

OBJECTIVES

- Build an understanding of group conversations and the role they play in children's science learning
- Build various strategies for facilitating science talks
- Build an awareness of what inhibits conversations

OVERVIEW

- Provide overview of science talks (30 minutes)
- Help teachers analyze a small group science talk (25 minutes)
- Help teachers analyze a large group science talk (35 minutes)

INSTRUCTOR PREPARATION

- **GIVE ASSIGNMENT.** At least two weeks before the workshop, distribute the "Read and Reflect" assignment. Also ask teachers to pay attention as they talk with children, noting when they are succeeding and where they have difficulty.

- **REVIEW VIGNETTES.** View the vignettes, noting the aspects you will highlight during the workshop.

MATERIALS

- Video vignette 8: "Constructing a Wall" and vignette 9: "Group Sharing," VCR, and monitor
- Copies of handouts: vignette observation form, transcripts of vignettes 8 and 9, "Read and Reflect 13," and "Strategies for Facilitating Science Talks"
- Charts: "Strategies for Science Talks" and "Issues We Are Having with Science Talks"
- Overhead projector, screen, and overheads 13.1–13.3

Activity

OVERVIEW OF SCIENCE TALKS (30 MINUTES)

PURPOSE: This activity will set the stage for analyzing science conversations with young children. It will allow teachers to share their successes and issues, expand their repertoire of strategies, and begin to overcome barriers they may be experiencing.

1. **INTRODUCE THE WORKSHOP** and begin to identify strategies for promoting conversations with young builders (15 minutes). It will allow teachers to share their successes and issues, expand their repertoire of strategies, and begin to overcome barriers they may be experiencing.

a. Remind teachers of the importance of conversations in developing children's understandings. Review these points:

- Conversation stimulates and makes explicit the thinking processes that underlie several aspects of inquiry (such as collecting data, synthesizing and analyzing data, drawing conclusions, making theories, and using language to communicate). It is also an essential aspect of collaboration.

- Sharing ideas stimulates scientific activity among peers.

- Children's experiences and ideas are more easily recorded for future reference when they put words to their actions.

- In addition to the ways they benefit science learning, conversations build language capacity and promote early literacy.

b. For a few minutes, allow teachers to share successful strategies for facilitating science talks, as well as issues they have encountered. Use the posters you have made to record their comments and ideas. As they share, ask some questions: "Why do you say that strategy worked? What is the evidence of its success? How did it promote science inquiry and learning? How did the children respond?" Try to address the issues during the workshop.

2. **PROVIDE A FRAMEWORK FOR FURTHER DISCUSSION OF CONVERSATIONS** (15 minutes) using overheads 13.1–13.3. Start with important aspects of conversations that are science focused. Then introduce the idea that there are strategies to avoid. Finally, introduce the settings in which science conversations can occur.

OVERHEAD 13.1: FOCUS ON SCIENCE CONCEPTS BY PROMOTING INQUIRY

- **Responses that promote reflection**

    – *Restate or paraphrase a child's statement.*

    – *Ask children for their ideas, such as what they did to make their building strong or if it is as tall as it can be without falling.*

    – *Accept their ideas without judgment.*

Teachers can encourage children's reflection by listening carefully and restating without judgment. Teachers can also communicate that they value children's ideas by giving nonverbal cues such as head nods and verbal acknowledgments such as, "That's an interesting idea."

- **Responses that promote analysis**

    – *Ask for descriptive details.*

    – *Ask for examples, comparisons, and alternatives.*

    – *Ask, What if . . . ? Why do you think so? How do you know?*

Describing their observations sets the stage for analysis. When teachers ask why or how, they are probing for the evidence that underlies children's ideas.

OVERHEAD 13.2: RESPONSES THAT INHIBIT OR LIMIT THINKING

- **Responses that inhibit children's thinking**

  – *Explaining the phenomenon to the children*

  – *Cutting children off*

  – *Correcting or telling children what to think*

These are all common responses that teachers have been using for years. They will need to listen to themselves and work to replace these responses with some that encourage thinking.

- **Responses that limit children's thinking**

  – *Lead them to "correct" answer*

  – *Tell them what to do*

  – *Move on too quickly*

Teachers often respond using the "strategies" above, particularly the last one. It takes time to think, and we need to give children time before probing for further responses.

OVERHEAD 13.3: SETTINGS FOR SCIENCE CONVERSATIONS

- **Talks with small groups**
  This is an especially important strategy because small group science talks can involve everyone. This setting can be used to reflect on a building experience, what was learned and what it might mean, or to encourage collaborative problem solving and learning from others.

- **Talks with the whole group**
  Whole group science talks help children learn from others. Hearing what others have seen and done can help children reflect on their observations, while focusing their attention on the science of building. Data from multiple experiences can come together and support the analysis process. Various theories will come forward for comparison. At the same time, these science talks can give children ideas for how they can engage in future explorations, while engaging reluctant builders.

- **Talks featuring materials or documents at the center**
  With both large and small groups, it is important to bring the concrete into the setting. Building materials, photographs, representations, records of data—all help children connect with their investigations.

TALKING WITH SMALL GROUPS (25 MINUTES)

PURPOSE: This activity will help participants focus on the role of conversations in deepening children's thinking.

Reinforce ideas by viewing and discussing a small group science talk. Introduce vignette 8 by saying that it was taped in a kindergarten classroom in Boston. It features two children investigating a teacher's question. Give each teacher the vignette observation form for taking notes and the transcript.

After viewing the vignette, ask for teachers' observations, "How did this teacher use the talk to engage the children with inquiry and the science concepts?" Ask for specific examples of strategies and why she may have used them by asking, "What exactly did she say? Why do you think she did that?" Or, "What did that strategy provide for the children?"

Highlight the following points when discussing the vignette:

- Teacher defines the question being investigated: "What do you think she could do to keep that block standing up?"

- Teacher asks "Why do you think" questions to encourage reasoning.

- Teacher encourages Eddie's use of words to make his approach explicit.

- Teacher encourages Dierdre's close observation: "Okay, watch this, Dierdre. See how he's pushing the two sides together?"

- Teacher asks for a prediction: "You think if you blow it, it will fall?"

LARGE GROUP SCIENCE TALK (35 MINUTES)

PURPOSE: This is an opportunity for teachers to observe a large group science talk. The teacher facilitates teachers who are sharing recent building experiences and strategies being used to create stability. It is also an opportunity to focus on strategies that support participation of English language learners.

Support teachers' strategies by viewing and discussing a large group science talk. Introduce vignette 9 by saying that it was taped in a Head Start classroom in Boston. It features a teacher who is helping children share their recent building experience during whole group time. She is concerned about keeping the children too long, but the children keep the conversation going. Point out that most of these children are English language learners and that nine languages are spoken in the class. If your teachers also have English language learners in their classrooms, make a point of talking about the strategies being used that support their engagement (see box below). Distribute the transcript and ask teachers to take notes in the vignette 9 column of their observation form.

After viewing the vignette, ask for teachers' observations using the following questions to guide the conversation:

- What science concepts are being explored?

- What aspects of inquiry are these children engaged in? (You may want to refer to the inquiry diagram in the teacher's guide or by showing the overhead.)

- What strategies is the teacher using to deepen science understanding?

- What might she have done differently?

Highlight the following points when discussing the vignette:

- What science concepts are being explored?

  – Children are examining design strategies that provide stability when building tall.

- What aspects of inquiry are these children engaged in?

  – Reflection, interpreting data, close observation of the data in documents, sharing, and formulating ideas.

- What strategies is the teacher using to deepen science understanding?

  – Draws out varied ideas from several children.

  – Uses documentation (representation and photos) for reflection and analysis, as well as to help communicate ideas.

  – Encourages reasoning: "How do you think that one helps to make this one so it doesn't fall?" "Why do you think it might fall down?"

  – Provides for more focused investigation: "Maybe we should try building it and see what happens."

- What might she have done differently?

  – Ask for volunteers to investigate the new question.

  – Document the ideas shared about strategies for stability and make a documentation panel for future reference.

  – Ask Victor about how he stabilized the tall pieces in his submarine.

- Other points to make:

  – Another important goal is to get children to talk to one another. Encourage children to direct questions and comments to their peers when appropriate.

  – These conversations are hard to manage. Start with brief conversations and extend the length as children build their ability to attend. Use questions and comments to draw in children who may be getting restless.

When discussing the English language learners, highlight these strategies. Mention that these strategies support the participation, science engagement, and language development of all young children.

- Use body language to illustrate ideas being expressed.
- Restate with corrections—"That's the part that goes up to see the fishes."
- Build on each other's comments.
- Draw children back in by referring to their previous contributions, as the teacher does with Aria.

To conclude, pass out the strategies handout and let teachers know about the next workshop activities, and give them any assignment you want them to do.

Suggested Next Steps

Conducting science talks is a difficult skill for teachers to learn. It will be helpful if you can give them more support as they incorporate science talks into their practice.

- Both workshops on representation have examples of conversations with children that would help teachers build their skills in this area.

- Guided discussions are an excellent way to deepen teacher understanding of science talks. During these discussions, teachers can share video- or audiotape conversations from their classrooms and discuss them. Transcribing is time consuming, but a very effective form of documentation for these kinds of conversations.

- Mentoring is another excellent way to support teachers. Observe a conversation, document it, and then talk with the teacher about what she did, reinforcing the strategies she is using and brainstorming ideas for the missed opportunities.

TRANSCRIPT OF VIDEO VIGNETTE 8:
CONSTRUCTING A WALL

Scene: This Boston kindergarten teacher is facilitating some problem solving by encouraging Eddie to help Dierdre learn how to make a wall stand up.

Teacher: Can Eddie help us solve this problem? Dierdre is trying to figure out how to stand this block up.

(Dierdre working with large flat blocks.)

Dierdre: I'm trying to make this and this over the side.

Teacher: And it's not staying up. Every time she takes her hand off, that happens. What do you think she could do to keep that block standing up? Here, I'll let you sit down so you can do it.

(Eddie shows Dierdre how a block can stand up by placing supporting horizontal blocks.)

Dierdre: I need one more of these.

Teacher: Oh, it worked. Oh, you could even take that—oh. *(Dierdre keeps working on her wall.)* Now why isn't it staying up the way it stood up when Eddie did it? Can you tell her with your words what to do, Eddie? What does she need to do to keep that up? Tell her with your words. What does she need to do? You're using your hands. Another block there. Is there another block?

Dierdre: No more.

Teacher: There's no more over there. It's not staying up. Okay, Eddie. You want to show her one more time how to do it? Oh, watch your head. Okay, watch this, Dierdre. See how he's pushing the two sides together? And he lets it go and it stays up. It's staying up. Oh.

Eddie: I think if I blow it, it will fall.

Teacher: You think if you blow it, it will fall? Oh.

(Eddie blows on structure and it falls.)

Dierdre: Eddie.

Teacher: What if you put that other block back, Dierdre? You think if you blow it, it will fall?

Dierdre: Yes. No.

(Eddie blows on structure again and it falls.)

Teacher: You don't think so? Oh. It still falls down.

TRANSCRIPT OF VIDEO VIGNETTE 9:
GROUP SHARING

Scene: This Boston Head Start teacher is using a large group time for sharing of recent building experiences and successful strategies used.

Teacher: *(Points to drawing on easel)* Ikechukwu, tell us a little bit about this house that you made. It's very tall, isn't it?

Ikechukwu: Yes.

Teacher: It's very tall. Did it fall down? *(Using hand motions to help the children understand her word.)*

Ikechukwu: Not fall down.

Teacher: It didn't fall down. How did you make it stay up so tall?

Unidentified child: That tall.

Teacher: Aria, do you think that Ikechukwu balanced the blocks very carefully like you told me Armin did?

Aria: They put up a lot.

Teacher: He put them softly, gently on top of each other?

Aria: And soft. The block is on the block soft and it's staying.

Teacher: Okay, you know what? At playtime I want you to show me what you mean. I think I know. You know what, can you get two blocks right now and show us? Get two of the square ones, Victor—for Aria so—he can show us what he means. Yes—no. Victor, look at Mercedes—yes. Get Aria some of those. And Aria, can you stand up? Stand up and show us on top of the shelf what you mean when you say "put them soft." How do you put them soft?

Aria: *(Puts one block on top of another)* This soft.

Teacher: Soft. So that you mean the top one is exactly on top? Is that what you mean?

Aria: No. It sticks on the block.

Teacher: So it sticks on the block. Okay. Do you want to show us with a couple more? Can you take a few out and show us on top?

Aria: No.

Teacher: No, you don't want to. Okay. If you're ready to go . . . *(singing)*.

Armin: Can I use something?

Teacher: Sure. Armin wants to say one more thing before we go to play. Go ahead, Armin.

Armin: *(Points to drawing)* Ikechukwu put this there so it can't *(inaudible)*.

Teacher: Oh, Armin just said—he was really looking at the picture. He said do you see this little piece at the bottom that Ikechukwu put here? Armin said Ikechukwu put that there so that this one won't fall. Armin, how do you think that one helps to make this one so it doesn't fall? Does it kind of hold it? It holds it? I want to find out what Armin's thinking about.

Bertram: Falling. This is just *(inaudible)* there and this is going to hold all these.

Teacher: When these are start to fall . . .

Bertram: It will hold all these.

Teacher: The little one can hold it.

Armin: Ikechukwu put one of these and one of these so it can't fall anymore.

Teacher: That's a really great observation.

John Michael: The tall one might fall down.

Teacher: The tall one. You think your tall one might fall down?

John Michael: Ikechukwu's.

Teacher: Ikechukwu's. Why do you think it might fall down?

Bertram: Because he didn't put it straight.

Teacher: You know, I want to hear John Michael finish and then you tell us your idea.

John Michael: Because he put it that right there so, so that one can fall down.

Teacher: He put what one? Point to it on the picture and show me. Which one did he put so it can't fall?

John Michael: That one.

Teacher: That one. That's the one Armin was looking at.

John Michael: That one. And that pushed that one.

Teacher: And so you were afraid this will fall and push that one down. Yeah, it could. Maybe it could—I don't know. Maybe we should try building it and see what happens. Bertram, what were you going to say?

Bertram: This, I said, this he didn't put it straight.

Teacher: You don't think it's very straight.

Bertram: That's why it's going to fall.

Teacher: That's what Armin was talking—Aria was talking about, putting the blocks very, very straight on top of each other so they balance.

Child: Like John Michael's. John Michael's is straight.

Teacher: Yes, John Michael's looks very straight. We have lots and lots and lots of building we can do today.

Victor: (Inaudible; a reference to sharing his submarine.)

Teacher: (Holds up enlarged photograph.) Victor's submarine and James's submarine. Can we talk about it just for one more minute? Because it's so important, Victor and James. Can you come up here? Manuel, look at Victor and James's submarine. Can you tell us about the submarine that you and James made? Come over here so everyone can see it. Tell us about it.

Victor: This is where go to fishes.

Teacher: That's the part that goes up to see the fishes. Okay. And what about this part?

Victor: Goes to see the alligators.

Teacher: That goes to see the alligators. So how do the people see? How do the people see through that one?

Victor: Put that there and put that down.

Teacher: They're down here and they pull it down and they look? And then they look all the way up through that piece. Cool. Thank you. We're going to hang this one up too. We have lots and lots of building today. Again, we have—James, can you find a spot? We have foam blocks over on the table. The blue ones. We're going to have unit blocks in the block area. We're going to have hollow blocks in this area. We're going to have our little wooden blocks.

ADVANCED WORKSHOP 13: VIGNETTE OBSERVATION FORM

Note your observations by identifying the teacher strategies and child responses for each vignette.

Vignette 8	Vignette 9

STRATEGIES FOR FACILITATING SCIENCE TALKS

1. Start slowly. For example, you might begin with five- to ten-minute conversations and increase the time as children increase their engagement. Take cues from the children to decide when to stop and when to continue.

2. Choose a concrete stimulus for the conversation. For example, you might choose an actual building or structure, a child's drawing or photograph of a building or structure, or a picture from a book.

3. Be enthusiastic and curious. For example, "I am so excited about what happened this morning. Who wants to talk about the structure they built?"

4. Model ways of sharing your thoughts and some of the questions you have. For example, "I was wondering if there was a way to build doors that open and close on your houses."

5. Expand on children's observations and ideas. For example, if Jamilla says, "I saw pretty windows," you might rephrase her statement to be more descriptive by saying something like, "Jamilla remembers seeing the stained glass windows on the front of the church."

6. Ask questions to engage children in analysis. For example, "Why do you think your building fell when you put the long block on top? Is there a different block that might work better? Why do you think it will work?"

7. Ask questions to help children predict. For example, "Which kind of blocks do you think will make the best foundation for your skyscraper? Why do you think so?" Be sure to follow by asking why they think so or by getting them to compare different responses.

8. Provide children with the support they need to share their thoughts about the following:
   - Give children time to think before you expect them to respond. Silent time is okay.
   - Find ways for children with limited language and second language learners to demonstrate what they know.
   - Model using descriptive language by explaining a child's actions. For example, "I see you are placing those blocks very carefully on each other."

9. Draw out ideas. For example, "Tommy showed us how he made a window in his house. Can someone show us a different way to do it?"

10. Avoid comments that inhibit or limit thinking. Avoid the following:
    - Explaining the science phenomena yourself
    - Correcting children
    - Leading them to the "correct" answer
    - Moving on too quickly

READ AND REFLECT 13

In preparation for advanced workshop 13, review "The Teacher's Role" (pp. 75–77) in "Resources." This section provides advice for facilitating science talks. Find guidance for conducting science talks in the open exploration or focused exploration sections of the guide. Note ideas from the guide that you would like to try below. Facilitate a few small and large group science talks using suggestions for your reading. Note the children's engagement and participation, and complete the reflection questions below. You may want to record a few conversations on audiotape for later reflection.

1. Ideas to try:

2. Successful strategies:

3. Difficulties:

ADVANCED WORKSHOP 14

Making and Using Documentation Panels

At a Glance

Purpose:
- Learn about the role documentation panels play in science explorations
- Learn to make and evaluate panels
- Learn to use panels to help children revisit, reflect on, and extend their work

Activity	Time	Materials
Introduce documentation panels Present an overview of the "what" and "why" of documentation panels. Guide teachers as they examine a sample panel.	35 minutes	• Overhead projector, screen, and overheads 14.1–14.5 • Copies of overhead 14.1 for small groups to look at
Help teachers make documentation panels Support teachers as they use documents they have brought from their classrooms to make panels that illustrate a recent science exploration. Ask them to use the criteria to evaluate their own panels and share their learning.	1 hour	• Overhead projector, screen, and overhead 14.6 • Poster-making supplies • Copies of documentation panel feedback form

Preassignment: Read "Guidelines for Creating Documentation Panels" in the teacher's guide (p. 92). Complete workshop 14 assignment.

Advanced Workshop 14:
Making and Using Documentation Panels

OBJECTIVES

- Learn about the role documentation panels play in science exploration
- Learn to make and evaluate panels
- Learn to use panels to help children revisit, reflect on, and extend their work

OVERVIEW

- Introduce documentation panels (30 minutes)
- Help teachers make documentation panels (1 hour)

INSTRUCTOR PREPARATION

- **DISTRIBUTE ASSIGNMENT.** At least a week before the workshop, give teachers the workshop 14 assignment. Also tell teachers to read the guidelines for creating documentation panels in the teacher's guide.

MATERIALS

- Overhead projector, screen, and overheads 14.1–14.6
- Poster-making supplies including oaktag, rubber cement, markers, assorted colored paper, scissors
- Copies of handouts: overhead 14.1, documentation panel feedback form, workshop 14 assignment

Activity

INTRODUCTION TO DOCUMENTATION PANELS (35 MINUTES)

PURPOSE: This discussion provides the essential information about panels—what are they, why they are important, and how to use them.

1. **INTRODUCE THE WORKSHOP** (5 minutes) by telling teachers they will be focusing on a practical skill for the next hour and a half—making documentation panels. At the same time, teachers will see how this process triggers valuable ideas about their work. Confirm that everyone has brought documents for making panels. Pair anyone who did not bring documents with someone who did.

2. **PROVIDE AN OVERVIEW OF THE VALUE OF PANELS** (20 minutes). Connect panels to science learning by showing and discussing the following slide sequence:

   a. Remind participants of the science goals by reviewing overheads 1.2 and 1.3 and by referring them to the outcomes in the teacher's guide on p. 97. Tell teachers that the main goal of documentation panels is to make the science learning visible. Highlighting children's engagement with science processes and ideas is key.

b. Ask participants to form groups of three. Give each group a copy of overhead 14.1 (a documentation panel). Show overhead 14.2, and review the questions they will use to guide their discussion. Leave the overhead up while they talk.

OVERHEAD 14.2: DOCUMENTATION PANEL DISCUSSION QUESTIONS

- **What is the intended message in this panel? What is the teacher trying to communicate?**
Look for ideas such as the teacher wanted to show the children's process of inquiry and the learning that came from it. The photos provide a new perspective for the children, allowing them to see themselves next to their towers.

- **Where is the science engagement and learning in this panel?**
Look for ideas such as ability to consider the characteristics of materials as well as design strategies and how effective they are for building stable towers. They are engaged in a focused exploration, use their bodies to measure height, and analyze their work to form ideas about design.

- **How well are these messages communicated? Where is the evidence of children's science learning?**
Look for ideas such as the use of photos and captions to convey the inquiry process and reflect the children's science ideas.

- **How would you change this panel?**
There might be a reference to the period of time represented on the panel. Some of the pictures may have been taken closer to the action. Teachers may have other ideas too. The question will help them think analytically and identify new approaches.

---

c. After ten minutes, show overhead 14.1 and discuss teachers' responses to each question. If you have time, show overhead 14.3. Tell teachers that while the previous documentation panel focused on a challenge a group of children participated in, this focuses on collaboration in problem solving and introduces a question that asks for close observation of the photographs.

You may want to read aloud the teacher's commentary that appears at the bottom of the documentation panel:

Left side: James said he would show Despina and Ursile how to do it so it wouldn't fall down. What is he doing differently? (Look at the pieces going up.)

Right side: Theresa tried it the next day. Look at her pieces going up. Tell me about it.

Use the questions on overhead 14.2 to discuss participants' reactions.

Look for ideas like these:

- What is the intended message in this panel?
  This is a simple panel that is focused on one building strategy. It highlights collaboration.

- Where is the science engagement and learning in this panel?
  The children are focused on ways to create stability while using long blocks vertically.

- How well are these messages communicated?
  The photos illustrate two approaches: the girl's less successful approach and James's more stable structure. The text focuses your attention when examining the photos.

- How would you change this panel?
  Give teachers a chance to share some ideas they have.

3. **ASK TEACHERS HOW THEY WOULD DESCRIBE A DOCUMENTATION PANEL** (5 minutes). You might ask: "How might we define documentation panel?" Discuss a few ideas, then show and review overhead 14.4.

OVERHEAD 14.4: WHAT IS A SCIENCE-FOCUSED DOCUMENTATION PANEL?

- **A visual display that illustrates science inquiry and learning**
  Share that the real benefit of documentation panels is that they make the process of inquiry and learning visible to teachers, children, and families.

- **A multimedia presentation**
  Explain that a combination of text, photos, and work samples can capture the complexity of the process in which children are engaged. As teachers learn to create panels they will also learn to evaluate the quality of each document they use—which photos actually illustrate engagement and science learning, which representations reveal science understandings, and which quotes from the children communicate important science ideas. Over time, teachers' understanding of science and children's learning deepen as they repeatedly engage in this process.

- **A story that can either take place over time or at one point in time**
  Mention that documentation panels can illustrate one activity or a sequence of activities. Panels that have a narrow focus are more useful in working with the children, but panels that span a longer period of time can help teachers evaluate their teaching. Then, they can look for connections from one activity to the next.

---

4. **REVIEW THE USES OF DOCUMENTATION PANELS** (5 minutes) by asking teachers how they might use them. After listening to their ideas for a few minutes, show overhead 14.5.

OVERHEAD 14.5: USES OF DOCUMENTATION PANELS

- **A stimulus for science talks**
  The documentation panel helps children share what they have done with others. It can also be posted in the room for all of the children to refer to as they move forward in their exploration.

- **An opportunity to promote literacy as well as science**
  Children are eager to "read" their own stories and will learn a lot from the process of "reading" panels.

- **Educate families**
  Panels on display provide families with insights into what children are doing and the science they are learning. Keep families and your colleagues in mind as potential audiences for documentation panels.

- **Teacher reflection**
  The process of making the panel is a valuable opportunity for teachers to reflect on their work and consider next steps to take with these children and the whole group.

MAKING DOCUMENTATION PANELS (1 HOUR)

PURPOSE: This activity allows participants to reflect on the science teaching and learning in their classroom as they learn to create a panel that they can use with children and families.

1. **INTRODUCE THE ACTIVITY** (10 minutes) by telling teachers that they will now have a chance to make a panel. Show overhead 14.6 as a review.

OVERHEAD 14.6: MAKING DOCUMENTATION PANELS

- **Identify a science exploration focus to illustrate**
  Keep science concept(s) and inquiry skill(s) at the forefront of your message. You might focus on ideas children have about building materials or strategies for building strong and stable, the results of a challenge, data collected, or ideas generated by comparing data (such as the measurement of different towers), to name a few.

- **Collect documents that will help tell your story**
  Collect work samples, photographs, dialogue, and observational notes that tell the story.

- **Arrange documents on posterboard**
  Arrange documents left to right and in chronological order. When you are satisfied with the arrangement, glue them down and add captions.

- **Add a title that focuses on your readers**
  Be sure your title communicates your key message.

Review the available materials (oaktag, rubber cement, markers, and so on). Tell teachers that their task is to organize a presentation of the documents they have brought. Remind them to add captions that explain what is shown in the photos and work samples.

Suggest they open their teacher's guides to the science outcomes chart. Tell teachers that they can use this chart to highlight how children used the inquiry skills or explored different science concepts.

Instructor's Notes:

Watch out! Creating documentation panels is sometimes considered an appropriate place for teacher decorations. You may need to remind some that this is about science learning and that decorations can detract from the important message about the children's engagement and learning.

Allow twenty-five minutes to lay out panels.

2. **SUPPORT THEIR WORK** (25 minutes) by wandering around the room. Answer questions and listen to their discussion to be sure they are on track and moving ahead.

3. **ASK THEM TO USE THE CRITERIA** (15 minutes) on the documentation panel feedback form to evaluate their own panel. Pass out the forms and let teachers know that they can continue to work on their panel. However, while they are working, they should consider how well their panel meets the criteria. Join in these discussions as you move around the room, sharing your own thoughts. Let them know when you will bring them together. It is not essential that they finish their panels—they can always do it after the workshop. If some finish early, encourage them to wander around and look at what others have done.

4. **BRING THEM TOGETHER FOR FINAL COMMENTS** after 10 minutes. Ask a few groups to comment on particular decisions they made that highlight the process and the different approaches they have taken. You might want to ask what they learned from considering the criteria and what they would do differently next time. Other possible discussion questions might include the following:

   - Which inquiry skill(s) did you decide to focus on? Why? How did you decide on the concept?

   - While making your panel, what have you learned about science teaching and learning? Keep teachers focused on their own panel and what they might have learned about the children or their own teaching as they reflected on the documents.

   - What did you learn by looking at other panels? Again, keep the focus on children's engagement and learning and on the teacher's role. If teachers have obviously benefited by sharing their work, encourage them to think about how they can continue to do this. Suggest that in addition to sharing panels, they can also share and discuss photographs, children's work samples, or audiotaped conversations.

   - How might you use this panel with your children? Ask, "What do you hope the children will gain?" Look for ideas such as, "I would take the panel to a science talk to help children share what they did with the others, and I would post it in the room so others can refer to it." Such activities can stimulate children's thinking and help them revisit and build on their ideas and experiences, as well as those of others.

In closing, encourage teachers to share their panels and to use them with children and families. Remind them when and where the next workshop or study group is and what they need to do to prepare.

Suggested Next Steps

- Follow up with teachers, asking how they are using panels in their classrooms. Have they displayed them at child's eye level? Did they use them to encourage a science talk? How did it go?

- Offer the workshop on science talks or using children's representations as teaching tools, which will give teachers ideas about how to use the panels to stimulate conversations.

- Focus a few guided discussions on the use of panels with children, allowing teachers to share and analyze their experiences.

- Offer to help teachers who are interested in forming a documentation panel group. Provide a space, supplies, and tools for them to use when they get together to make panels.

DOCUMENTATION PANEL FEEDBACK FORM

Name: _____

Panel: _____

Use the following criteria as you consider the panel's effectiveness:

- Is the science content, with which the children were engaged, evident? What is it? Where is the evidence?

- Is children's inquiry process evident? What is it? Where is the evidence?

- Does the panel provide important background information? Do you understand what you need to know about the setting, timing, and what the children were doing?

- How well do photographs capture children's engagement and actions?

- How well do the work samples and quotes illustrate the important message about science engagement and learning?

- One thing that is really good about this panel:

- One suggestion for improvement:

ADVANCED WORKSHOP 14 ASSIGNMENT

1. Read the section about documentation panels on p. 92 in the teacher's guide. Review the curriculum and look for places where the directions ask you to make a documentation panel.

2. Identify an aspect of children's exploration that you would like to document.

3. Collect a set of three or four documents that you can use to create a panel that reflects children's engagement in science inquiry. Use the following guidelines when collecting:
   - Documents should all be related to a particular aspect of your exploration. For example, they might be about strategies for building strong towers or an investigation of materials to use for roofs.
   - The document should be varied, including some or all of the following: children's drawings or paintings, photos of three-dimensional representations, photos of children engaged in the exploration, quotes from their conversation, predictions, and conclusions.

THE CULTURE OF INQUIRY

- An emphasis on the importance of building structures

- An emphasis on inquiry

- Sharing observations and ideas

- Recording observations and experiences

THE SCIENCE TEACHER'S GOALS

- Encourage children to build structures

- Guide children's inquiry

- Deepen children's science understanding

SCIENCE TEACHING AND LEARNING

- Young children develop ideas about science from their life experiences.

- New experiences lead children to challenge previous naïve ideas.

- A balance between exploration and thinking, reasoning, and theorizing provides a strong basis for learning.

- Inquiry that leads to science learning takes time.

- When guided, children have the ability to engage in all aspects of the inquiry process.

KEY IDEAS ABOUT THIS APPROACH TO SCIENCE LEARNING

• Building understanding of important science concepts is an appropriate goal for young children.

• Children naturally form ideas about the world based on their life experiences.

• In inquiry-based science our role is to provide new experiences that can lead children to more sophisticated theories.

"Experience is not the best teacher.
It sounds like heresy, but when you think about it, it's reflection on experience that makes it educational."

—George Forman,
Professor Emeritus, University of Massachusetts

SCIENCE BOOKS AND SCIENCE LEARNING

- Stimulate science inquiry and thinking

- Provide images and examples of careers in science

- Provide information and ideas relevant to children's scientific inquiries

- Connect science exploration with the world outside the classroom

- Introduce children to the way building science appears in many different kinds of books

SCIENCE BOOKS AND LITERACY DEVELOPMENT

- Build language skills

- Introduce many genres of books about science

- Engage children with print

- Develop a love of books

USES OF BOOKS ABOUT BUILDING

- To refer to when building

- To read aloud and discuss

- To read aloud as introduction to a new idea or challenge

- To look at and talk about

KEY ELEMENTS OF ASSESSMENT PROCESS

- Collecting data

- Analyzing data regularly

- Drawing conclusions and making decisions

PABLO'S TOWER

Pablo

"If it only had one it would tilt."

I Be bedeingatang

Patrick's Kapla Tower

Picture is as big
as the tower.

Monet's Bridge

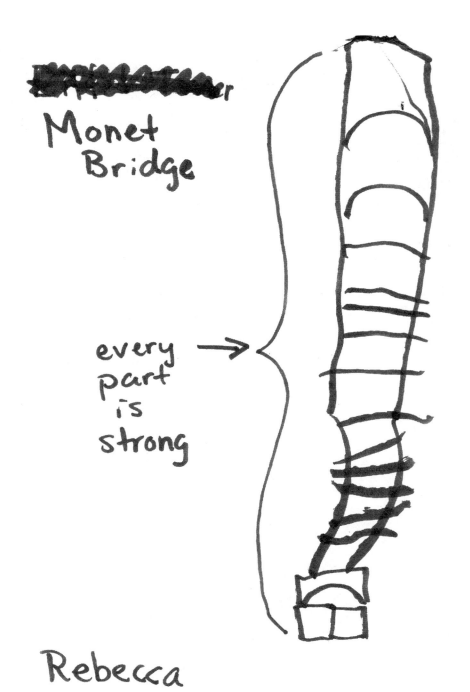

Monet
Bridge

every
part
is
strong

Rebecca

KATHARINE'S EIFFEL TOWER

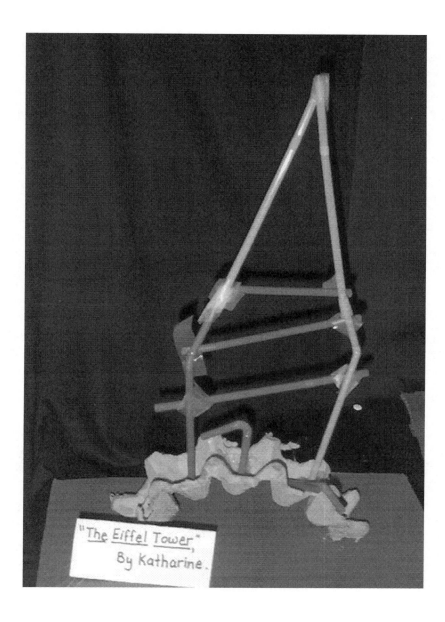

CHIDEMMA'S TOWER

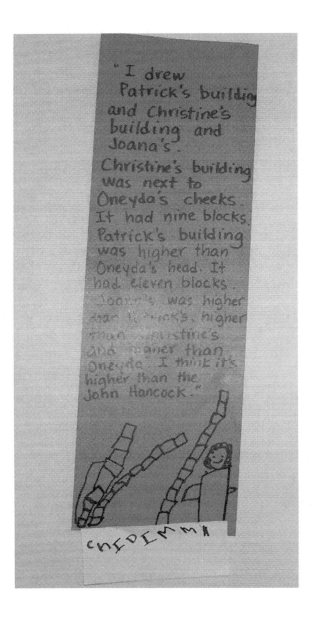

"I drew Patrick's building and Christine's building and Joana's. Christine's building was next to Oneyda's cheeks. It had nine blocks. Patrick's building was higher than Oneyda's head. It had eleven blocks. Joana's was higher than Patrick's, higher than Christine's and higher than Oneyda. I think it's higher than the John Hancock."

THREE-DIMENSIONAL COLLAGE

SAMPLE DOCUMENT ANNOTATION

DOCUMENT ANNOTATION

Child(ren): Gwen   **Date:** 5/9/01

Science being explored: Characteristics of objects and characteristics of materials

objects are made from

Inquiry skills being used: Synthesizes and analyzes data from experiences

Use Representations to Deepen Learning and Promote Inquiry

- Build ability to communicate observations and ideas

- Focus on particular science ideas

- Build a culture of inquiry and collaboration

- Connect children's explorations from one day to the next

- Recap what has been learned at key points in an exploration

- Stimulate discussion in which children synthesize and analyze their work

FOCUS ON SCIENCE CONCEPTS BY PROMOTING INQUIRY

• Responses that promote reflection

• Responses that promote analysis

RESPONSES THAT INHIBIT OR LIMIT THINKING

- Responses that inhibit children's thinking

- Responses that limit children's thinking

Settings for Science Conversations

- Talks with small groups

- Talks with the whole group

- Talks with materials or documents at the center

Documentation Panel

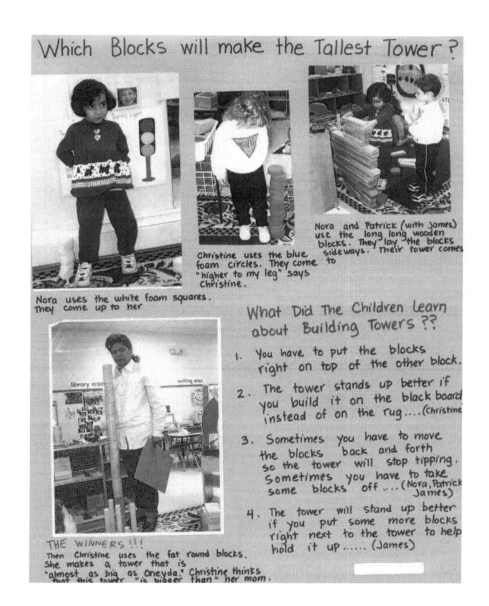

Which Blocks will make the Tallest Tower?

Nora uses the white foam squares. They come up to her

Christine uses the blue foam circles. They come "higher to my leg" says Christine.

Nora and Patrick (with James) use the long long wooden blocks. They lay the blocks sideways. Their tower comes to

THE WINNERS!!!
Then Christine uses the fat round blocks. She makes a tower that is "almost as big as Oneyda." Christine thinks that this tower "is bigger than" her mom.

What Did The Children Learn about Building Towers??

1. You have to put the blocks right on top of the other block.

2. The tower stands up better if you build it on the black board instead of on the rug....(Christine)

3. Sometimes you have to move the blocks back and forth so the tower will stop tipping. Sometimes you have to take some blocks off....(Nora, Patrick, James)

4. The tower will stand up better if you put some more blocks right next to the tower to help hold it up......(James)

DOCUMENTATION PANEL DISCUSSION QUESTIONS

- What is the intended message in this panel?
  What is the teacher trying to communicate?

- Where is the science engagement and learning in this panel?

- How well are these messages communicated?
  Where is the evidence of children's science learning?

- How would you change this panel?

DOCUMENTATION PANEL

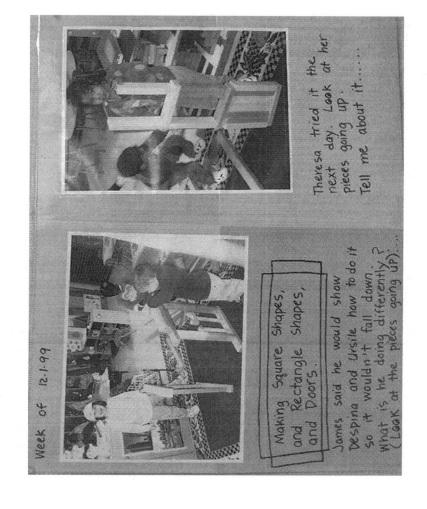

Week of 12.1.99

Making Square Shapes,
and Rectangle Shapes,
and Doors.

James said he would show
Despina and Ursile how to do it
so it wouldn't fall down.
What is he doing differently?
(Look at the pieces going up)....

Theresa tried it the
next day. Look at her
pieces going up.
Tell me about it......

What Is a Science-Focused Documentation Panel?

- A poster that illustrates science inquiry and learning

- A multimedia presentation

- A story that can either take place over time or at one point in time

Uses of Documentation Panels

- Stimulate science talks

- Promote literacy as well as science

- Educate families

- Promote teacher and child reflection

MAKING DOCUMENTATION PANELS

- Identify a science exploration focus to illustrate

- Collect documents that will help tell stories

- Arrange documents on posterboard

- Add a title that focuses your readers

guided discussions

Whether teachers are just beginning to use *Building Structures with Young Children* or are refining their practices as science teachers, you can use guided discussions to provide ongoing support and build collaboration among teachers. Through collaborative analysis of various materials, teachers build a deeper understanding of the science teaching and learning in their classrooms. By provoking inquiry and reflection, guided discussions support teachers as they engage in the ongoing process of refining their approach to teaching science. Guided discussions have the following advantages:

- **IMPROVE SCIENCE TEACHING AND LEARNING**
  These analytical discussions help teachers understand their role as science teachers and develop appropriate expectations for their children. Over time they develop a better understanding of the connections between their teaching and children's science learning. Improved practice is reinforced by child engagement and learning.

- **CREATE A COMMUNITY OF ADULT LEARNERS**
  Working in isolation, teachers often feel overwhelmed and very alone. By providing time and creating a structure for collaboration, teachers can share their resources and energy, while gaining a greater sense of community. This kind of support system encourages teachers to try out new ideas, share their experiences, and learn from others.

Once they have participated in the basic workshops, the guided discussions will keep enthusiasm alive, while supporting the implementation of "Building Structures with Young Children" in each teacher's classrooms. Guided discussions have some common elements, which include the following:

- A group of teachers who are motivated to explore the approach found in *Building Structures with Young Children* and to talk about how it relates to their practice and to children's learning

- A leader who has identified learning objectives and is willing to commit to the group and its development

- Documentation from teachers' classrooms (including video clips or observations of teaching practice, child work samples, or audiotaped conversations) to serve as common discussion points in group meetings

- A set of questions designed to guide the discussion, build connections between this approach and the documentation being used, help teachers reflect on their practice, and develop ways to apply new ideas to their work

Your guided discussions will be most successful under the following conditions:

- Discussions involve a small group of teachers (four to seven is optimal)

- Attendance is seen as part of teachers' regular responsibilities

- Time—an hour or hour and a half—is set aside regularly (at least monthly) for the discussions

- Discussions have a focus on practical aspects of science teaching and are structured so one builds on another

- A supervisor, mentor teacher, or other program leader is committed to planning and facilitating all of the discussions

- Leadership within the group is cultivated and the group becomes more self-sustaining

Selecting the right time to introduce guided discussions is also key to their effectiveness. They can be introduced at several points:

- **AFTER THE BASIC WORKSHOPS.** If you are working with a small group of teachers and want to move to a more informal setting after the basic workshops, consider starting guided discussions. Teachers will probably benefit from continual examination of the teacher's guide if they can focus on the stage of the teaching framework where they are currently working, either open exploration or focused exploration. Rereading sections of the teacher's guide, reviewing vignettes and work samples from the basic workshops, and sharing observations from their classroom will help them as they translate the print curriculum into their daily classroom life.

- **AFTER EACH ADVANCED WORKSHOP.** Guided discussions might also be offered in between the workshops with a specific focus on the teacher's application of the content from the workshop. In this approach, ongoing guided discussions are interrupted by workshops that provide new content. For example, if participants explored deepening children's science understanding in their last workshop, they might view a videotape from one of their classrooms, analyzing the children's engagement and considering possible next steps. Or they might read and discuss one of the articles recommended in the "Next Steps" box. One or two teachers can be responsible for sharing their classroom experience in each guided discussion. Stay on a topic for as many sessions as it takes for each teacher to discuss her work. Over time, teachers will begin to take some responsibility for planning the discussions. They will select topics, provide stimulus material, and plan discussion questions. They might select a focus that relates to their role as a facilitator of inquiry, such as encouraging representation or guiding science talks. Or they may want to better understand how to assess different kinds of child work by developing their observation skills or jointly examining work samples and transcripts.

Preparing for Guided Discussions

A successful guided discussion begins with thoughtful preparation. You will want to start by identifying teachers' needs and interests and then determining appropriate goals, materials, and questions. For teachers who have participated only in the basic workshops, these discussions can provide a more in-depth look at the teacher's guide, a more thorough discussion of some of the video vignettes and work samples used in the basic workshops, and time to explore emerging issues on documenting children's work. Try not to let the focus shift to control issues in the classroom. These group discussions are about the teaching and learning of science. Remind teachers of this and suggest another forum for the other topics they bring up.

Teachers who have participated in the advanced workshops can examine their own documents, which will stimulate and guide their reflection as they adopt new approaches and will provide a vehicle for ongoing support and collaboration.

Use the "Sample Guided Discussion Plans" in "Resources" (p. 199) when you begin to prepare your meetings. These sample plans provide goals, recommended materials, and discussion questions for three different kinds of discussions. Copy and use the planning form to record your plans and reflections for each discussion.

Use the following guidance to ensure the success of your discussions.

ASSESS TEACHERS' NEEDS

As you plan when and how to use guided discussions, you will need to take into consideration the teachers' backgrounds with curriculum and science teaching and the amount of previous experience they have had with "Building Structures with Young Children." Some teachers may have a background in science or your program might be using a curriculum that embraces the same teaching approaches. These teachers might more quickly grasp the approach to science and science teaching, and they might be ready to share more sophisticated insights and their own experiences in a self-directed setting. Teachers without this background will need a more intensive introduction to the teacher's guide first. Use the "Science Teacher Development Stages" in the section on assessing teacher growth (p. 204) to determine appropriate goals for teachers.

An essential aspect of their work as science teachers will be elevating the science content in the children's explorations. They must understand these science concepts in order to recognize them in their children's work. After their hands-on experiences with these concepts in the basic workshops, the guided discussions are a great place to reinforce what teachers understand. Always talk about the science that is present in the documents being discussed, the concepts they are exploring, and what they understand.

It is also important to consider teachers' own perceptions of their needs. As you conduct the workshops, listen carefully to their questions and concerns. Provide opportunities for them to suggest topics they want to focus on. If they have particular interests, their motivation to participate will be high.

DEVELOP A GOAL THAT RESPONDS TO TEACHERS' NEEDS

A goal is stated in broad terms and reflects one aspect of the approach found in *Building Structures with Young Children* (such as to better understand how children use representation to deepen their understanding of science ideas). Use the "Science Teacher Development Stages" on p. 204 as you think about appropriate goals for teachers. Also remember to take their interests into consideration. It will probably take several guided discussion meetings to fully explore one goal, as there will often be multiple perspectives to explore and you will want each teacher to have time to discuss her classroom.

DEVELOP LEARNING OBJECTIVES FOR EACH GOAL

Learning objectives provide more specificity than the goal. That is, objectives elucidate the goal by articulating the major points that you want teachers to take away from the discussion. Each goal might have several objectives. For example, if your goal is to better understand why representation is important to science learning, three objectives might be the following: (1) recognizing children's science ideas in their representations, (2) understanding the relationship between media being used (drawing, clay, three-dimensional collage) and the qualities of children's representations, and (3) exploring the role the teacher can play in encouraging representation and using it to deepen learning. It is the objective that will determine the content focus, the appropriate materials to use, and your guiding questions.

SELECT MATERIALS

Select material that will illustrate the learning objectives and fuel discussion. Whether you select a video clip, a section of the teacher's guide, children's work samples, or a reading recommended in the bibliography, the resource you select should achieve the following:

- Challenge teachers' previous notions about science teaching and learning. (These types of resources are more likely to provoke discussion than information that confirms what teachers already know.)

- Clearly illustrate children's engagement and science understandings, as well as the learning objective you have developed.

- If using a video, feature a situation that represents an aspect of the *Building Structures with Young Children* curriculum.

- If using a reading or case study, select one that contains relevant content written at a level appropriate for the teachers in the group.

As you prepare, become thoroughly familiar with the material. Consider the main message that the document conveys, how these ideas compare with teachers' current thoughts or practices, and how different teachers might respond.

DEVELOP DISCUSSION QUESTIONS

Develop discussion questions that will stimulate analysis of key points and practices. Create a core group of questions and a set of subquestions to raise if central points are missed during the discussion. Identify questions that will guide the discussion carefully from being descriptive to being analytical by following these four steps:

1. **BEGIN WITH GENERAL OPEN-ENDED QUESTIONS** about the document (such as, "What did you think about the article we read?").

2. **ASK FOR OBJECTIVE DESCRIPTION OF THE MATERIAL** (such as, "What do you see in this work sample? How would you describe its key features?"). Or you might ask teachers to take observational notes when watching a videotape and then review what they saw.

3. **ASK TEACHERS TO DRAW INFERENCES,** analyzing what they have seen by making connections between the stimulus and the content ideas (such as, "What exactly did this teacher do to encourage the conversation? What was the connection between the teacher's actions and the children's engagement? Did you see missed opportunities? What might you have

done differently?"). Always include some discussion of the children's science knowledge to reinforce the teachers' attention to the science concepts.

4. **FINALLY, ASK THEM TO DRAW CONCLUSIONS,** making connections to their own teaching (such as, "What connections can you make to the work you are doing in your classroom? Which of the approaches used here might work with your children? Which ideas generated by the group are worth trying?").

HELP PARTICIPANTS PREPARE FOR THE DISCUSSION

The teachers in your guided discussions can also prepare. You can help them by doing the following:

- Provide teachers with information about the content you will focus on beforehand to promote more thoughtful reflection. (For example, you might want them to read a portion of the teacher's guide or a related article or book chapter.)

- Share discussion questions, if you have them prepared.

Leading Guided Discussions

LAY THE GROUNDWORK IN THE FIRST MEETING

At your first meeting, spend some time as a group establishing the ground rules. Agree on a time limit and times to meet—keep in mind that regularly scheduled discussions have maximum impact. Ensure that the group knows that they are to listen respectfully to what others are saying and not interrupt. And let teachers know that a successful discussion depends more on what they have to say than on what you say. Rather, your role is to stimulate the discussion, keep the focus on science, summarize the group's thinking, and create bridges to the next level of questions.

FOLLOW THIS THREE-PHASE PROCESS WHEN FACILITATING GROUP MEETINGS

Phase 1: Open the meeting by briefly describing the content that is the focus for this discussion. For example, you might be examining a particular section of the teacher's guide or an aspect of the teachers' role. If you asked teachers to read a section of the guide or a related article before they came, provide time for them to share what they learned from the reading and list their ideas on a chart for later reference. Add to their list any important points that haven't come up yet. Explicit presentation of the relevant teaching and learning content is necessary for thoughtful analysis.

Phase 2: Introduce and review the materials you will use for the discussion. Briefly introduce the material and its purpose, connecting it back to the content you have just reviewed. For example, if you are working on developing the ability to engage children in conversations, and teachers will be analyzing a videotape of a science talk, introduce the viewing by asking teachers to focus on the strategies that you have just reviewed with them. Teachers will tune in differently and ask different questions depending on how you focus their attention. If your document is print materials, such as children's drawings or a series of photographs, try to have several sets so everyone can easily review them.

Phase 3: Guide the discussion using the questions that you developed to help the group fully explore important points. Remember the four steps that guide question development:

(1) begin with general, open-ended questions, (2) ask for objective descriptions, (3) draw inferences, and (4) draw conclusions. Leave a few minutes to summarize key points by distilling the thoughts and responses of teachers into several key points.

KEEP THE DISCUSSION FOCUSED ON THE TOPIC

Use these tips to promote full participation:

- Listen carefully and monitor teachers' body language to stay aware of how the group is doing. If you are not sure, check in with a simple "How are you doing with the discussion?"

- Ensure that each teacher has a chance to speak. Engage reluctant participants by making eye contact with them and smiling. Let them know through your body language that they have your support when they are ready to speak.

- Discourage anyone from dominating the conversation by moving the question to another person or by saying, "Let's hear from someone else on that issue."

- Encourage teachers to speak to each other, "Marie, you look like you have a suggestion for Joan. Let her know what you are thinking." Some teachers may be tempted to direct their comments to you or to wait for your response.

- Provide time after you ask a question. Teachers need time to reflect and come up with a thoughtful response. Your silence will communicate that it is their turn to talk and that it is all right for them to take time to think.

- Challenge ideas without challenging a teacher personally.

Build Communication and Leadership among Teachers

FOLLOW UP WITH EACH TEACHER

Whether it is individually or in the next discussion, provide time for teachers to talk about how implementing these new ideas went in their classrooms. If you are addressing the same topic over several discussions, you will want to open discussions with some reporting on their successes and issues to set the stage for further dialogue. List issues on a chart and return them at the end to see what new implications might help address issues. If you regularly observe and have conferences with these teachers, these are ideal times to acknowledge the progress they have made and the impact they have on children's learning. At the same time, you can pinpoint ongoing issues that you might want to build into guided discussion goals in the future.

ENCOURAGE TEACHER LEADERSHIP

As teachers learn the culture and process for engaging in guided discussions, begin to give them responsibility for planning and facilitating.

- Support teachers as they learn to create documents of the teaching and learning in their classrooms. Provide equipment and help with videotaping and photographing. Interested community groups might help by making contributions for equipment or volunteering time to help in the classroom. Be sure teachers have varied materials for children's representation. Give them time to reflect and plan.

- Let teachers plan guided discussion meetings with you. Help them learn the questioning sequence as they use the guided discussion planning form.

- Take a supporting role as you give them responsibility for facilitating meetings. While you let them take the lead, be prepared to jump in if they want support. You might ask a question that redirects a conversation that is getting off track or move the focus from a teacher who is dominating the dialogue.

- Debrief with them after, allowing them to share their feelings and questions. Use the planning form reflection questions to guide the conversation.

promoting teacher growth through mentoring

The basic and advanced workshops and the guided discussions provide an effective social setting for learning about science teaching. Teachers will also benefit from individual attention that focuses on their own issues as they implement *Building Structures with Young Children* in their classrooms. A supervisor or mentor can play a critical role in providing this individualized support, helping teachers evaluate their efforts and build their capacity as science teachers.

The primary goal of mentoring is to guide teachers' development as science teachers through reflection on their practice. You will help them choose appropriate goals, document their work, analyze their practice, and modify their approach to science teaching and learning. Mentoring provides important opportunities to build teachers' ability to do these things:

- Understand the science concepts in the context of children's play, conversations, and representations.

- Evaluate the teaching strategies they are using and their impact on children's science engagement and learning.

- Examine documents from their classrooms (videotape, transcripts of conversations, children's work samples, photographs, and observational notes) for evidence of children's inquiry and science understandings, as well as evidence of teaching effectiveness.

- Make informed decisions about their next steps with children's inquiry.

Ideally, mentors understand early childhood development, the complex nature of inquiry-based science, and the science being taught, and are able to analyze classroom science events. Effective mentors serve as guides: they share what they see, their knowledge, and their expertise in an objective and positive manner, while challenging teachers' thoughts and pushing their practice to new levels of competence. A mentor might be a supervisor, a professional developer, or a teacher who has reached the stage of development where they are refining their knowledge.

Observation and conferences are probably the most important tools mentors have for providing individualized support to teachers. Documentation collected during classroom observations provides the basis for collaborative analysis of teaching and learning, as well as for planning the next steps. The mentor's understanding of the specific classroom context, gained through observation, is essential for guiding teacher reflection and self-assessment.

The outcomes of this work will contribute to the successful implementation of *Building Structures with Young Children*. To conduct effective observations and conferences, follow these four steps:

1. Establish development goals and objectives with each teacher.
2. Prepare for classroom observations.
3. Conduct classroom observations.
4. Discuss the observations.

Step 1: Establish Development Goals and Objectives with Each Teacher

Use the first visit to establish several development goals with each teacher. Select a goal to start with and develop a few specific objectives that will be the focus of the teacher's initial work and your observations. For example, teachers may want to work on their ability to facilitate science talks. Possible objectives might include asking open-ended questions or using strategies that encourage children's representational drawing. Use the following steps to develop goals that both you and the teacher agree on:

- Conduct an initial classroom observation using "Evaluating Science Teaching" from "Resources" in the teacher's guide (see p. 207). This will guide recording what you see when observing. Review the teacher development stages on p. 204 to help you determine which parts of the form would be most appropriate to use with each teacher.

- Ask the teacher to use the evaluation form to reflect on her teaching and think about her goals.

- Meet with the teacher. Elicit her thoughts and share your observations. Together, determine the goal and specific objectives using the teacher development plan (p. 212). Use one form for each goal.

Step 2: Prepare for Classroom Observations

Successful classroom observations begin with planning. As you arrange for your visits, assure teachers that the goal of these observations is to support their growth as science teachers, not to judge their teaching for a high-stakes evaluation.

- Schedule a time to observe. Arrange a time when the classroom activity is in line with the teacher's current objectives. For example, if the teacher is working on facilitating large group science talks, schedule your visit to gain a full picture of a large group conversation.

- Conduct a pre-observation conversation with the teacher. Whether on-site or on the phone, get some background information to guide your observation. This information will be crucial when you begin to examine the teaching and learning.

Find out the following:

- The teacher's specific goals for children's engagement and learning

- Aspects of inquiry she expects the children to be engaged in

- Teaching strategies she will use to encourage and guide children's inquiry

- What has led up to these particular goals and activities

- The progress she feels she has made and frustrations she might feel in achieving her current goal

- Documentation (videotape, audiotape, or photographs) that might help illustrate this observation, as well as the notes you will take

Step 3: Conduct Classroom Observations

Use these strategies to develop an approach to observation that effectively supports teacher development:

- Check in with the teacher when you arrive. Without disturbing the classroom activity, find out if there have been any changes in the teacher's plans. Unusual circumstances will influence the flow of the day and what you can achieve in your observation.

- Document what you see and hear. It will be important to have specific information from your observation when you have a conference with the teacher. Take careful notes on paper that has been set up with three columns: child behaviors/comments, teacher responses, my thoughts. Separating your objective information into the child and teacher columns will help you make connections between the two later on. The subjective reactions you note in the right-hand column will help you remember the outstanding events when you plan the conference. Photographs (especially in series), videotapes, and audiotapes all provide clear evidence of children's engagement and are excellent supplements to your notes.

- Remain open and friendly. The classroom will function at its best when you are viewed as a friend. While maintaining your focus, engage in brief interactions with the children who are curious about your presence. "I am here because I want to watch you play," is a good response. It shows an interest in the children while letting them know that it is their activity that you are most interested in. Your interactions with children might model a particular strategy or test its effectiveness, or it might help you gain a new understanding of a particular child or dynamic. If there is a difficult situation and an extra pair of hands is needed, pitch in and help. The teacher needs to know that you are there to support her.

Step 4: Discuss the Observations

Timely, objective feedback will play a key role in a teacher's growth over time. Plan the conference soon after the observation. The events of the day will be fresh in your mind and the teacher's if you set the conference for the same day or the next. When you meet, invite the teacher to bring additional documentation of the events you observed. Children's work samples, a documentation panel, class-made book, or a set of photographs can provide an additional lens into the teaching and learning in the classroom.

Many teachers have not had the benefit of individual support that is focused on their professional growth. They will need time to learn how the process works and that they can trust your confidence and intentions, especially if you are their supervisor. Start by letting them control the agenda for the conference. You might set the focus on *Building Structures with Young Children*. Then let them show you what is happening and talk about their accomplishments and the issues on their mind. Once they have overcome any defensiveness and have learned that you are a helpful resource, you can share your perceptions, ask more challenging questions, and involve them in goal setting.

Once you get under way, keep the science concepts and inquiry process in the foreground as you use the following process to guide the teacher's reflection:

- Reflect on the observation and plan the conference. Take time to prepare for the conference. Think about what you saw and heard in the classroom and about what it means for this teacher's development as a science teacher. In preparation, complete the "Science Teacher Observation Synthesis" form (see p. 211 in "Resources"). Note the highlights of the interactions you observed in the child and teacher column. Select the events that are related to points you want to make or to specific events you want the teacher to think about. Consider the questions and comments that will encourage teacher reflection and problem solving. Note them in the box at the bottom of the form. Take time to think through how the teacher might react and what your response will be.

- Review the goals of the observation. Review with the teacher the focus you both agreed on and how you structured your observation. Keep the conversation focused throughout the conference. It will be easy to slip into a conversation about a sick child or the teacher's stressful life, but these topics will only divert attention from the teacher's development as a science teacher. You will have to be the judge when circumstances are important enough to modify the agenda.

- Open with an opportunity for the teacher to comment. Establish the value you place on the teacher's thinking by asking the following questions: "What did you think about the activities I observed?" "Were you pleased with how things went?" "Did you think your goals for the children's engagement and science learning were achieved?" Listen carefully to the responses. The teacher's perspective will give important clues as to how you proceed.

- Share your observations. Start by acknowledging places where you agree with the teacher, making specific connections between the teaching you observed and children's responses. Note the places where your perceptions might differ.

- Use available documentation to describe and analyze the events observed. Any documentation you have is data that can be analyzed. Use these documents to illustrate the descriptive points you and the teacher are making. Note the discrepancies in your perceptions and the teacher's, and what stands out in the data. As you begin to analyze the observed events, consider any discrepancies, the teacher's goals for the children, and the focus of her work with you. You want the teacher to do most of the talking, synthesizing her own impressions and your observations in order to assess her growth and needs. Use statements and questions to guide her reflection. Consider pursuing the following:

  - What the data says about the focus of her work with you—"You are working on strategies for facilitating science talks. What strategies did you effectively use in this activity?" "Let's look at the data and see what the children's responses were." Proceed to analyze the teacher's strategies in relation to the children's responses.

  - What the data says about student engagement and learning—"Let's look at this information and think about the science concepts being explored." Once identified, ask about evidence of the children's interests, questions, and understandings in relation to those particular concepts. Create a picture of the children's current understandings, their questions, and particular interests.

  - What the data highlights or the discrepancies in your perceptions—"I was amazed to see how much more Margarita is talking. What do you think has contributed to her new ability to participate in science talks and to the vocabulary she is using?" "We seem to have different ideas about what these children understand about the stability of their structure. I would like to better understand your thinking. Can you show me some evidence? Have you written down any comments they have made?"

- Help the teacher plan the next steps for her teaching and the children's learning. Once you have analyzed the observation, it is time to think about the implications for her teaching. You will want her to determine her next steps with the children and what she will do next in relation to the objectives she is working on.

  Start with the following questions: "What do you think your next steps should be with these children? How can you extend this experience and build their science understanding? What would you want to accomplish with these strategies? Why do you think these are the right next steps? How will they elevate the science and promote inquiry?"

- Close with goal setting and planning. It is now time to plan the teacher's next professional development steps. Should she continue to work on this goal? It is best to stay with one focus for a while, allowing the teacher to fully integrate new strategies and experience their effect. When it is time to move on to a new goal, select appropriate objectives. Finally, plan a few activities that will help her move forward. You might give her an article to read or suggest a classroom for her to observe. Her plan might simply be trying new strategies in her classroom. Once plans are made, record them on a teacher development plan (p. 212 in "Resources"), synthesize the major points of the conversation, and schedule your follow-up.

resources

Key Instructional Strategies

As you conduct the basic and advanced workshops, you will use four key instructional strategies:

- Encourage exploration of building structures

- Facilitate reflection on the science in teachers' explorations

- Present content about science and science teaching

- Guide analysis of classroom documentation to create a bridge between theory and practice

When these strategies are interwoven throughout your training program, you will help teachers integrate the *Building Structures with Young Children* approach into their teaching practice. In these workshops exploration precedes the presentation of content so that teachers can connect the content to these recent experiences with building and inquiry. When the analysis follows the science and science teaching content, it provides opportunities to make the content presented practical.

Below we describe each strategy, providing a purpose for its use and guidelines to follow as you use them in your training program. In addition, you will find strategies for effectively using the video vignettes.

ENCOURAGE EXPLORATION

These hands-on experiences provide adults with the opportunity to engage in inquiry and model, at an adult level, the children's investigations and experiences with building. They provide direct experiences with inquiry-based teaching through an open exploration of building, focused investigations of towers and enclosures, representation, and data collection and analysis.

PURPOSE

- Review past experiences with building and draw connections to new understandings

- Experience the use of inquiry skills and science exploration in the same way the children will

- Begin to build understanding of the science concepts, the nature of inquiry, and the approach to teaching

GUIDANCE

- Your preparation is key to effective training. You will want to read the advance preparation instructions at the beginning of each workshop. The preparation will involve exploring with blocks and collecting the building materials for the exploration. Read "Step 1: Preparing Yourself—Science" in the teacher's guide (p. 13) to help you understand the concepts that are the focus of these building explorations.

- As you lead teacher-explorers, you will be modeling the approach to teaching described in the teacher's guide. Use that guide as a resource as you prepare and reflect on your teaching. In the instructions for the workshops you will find discussion questions and purpose statements that will help you maintain your participants' focus.

- The time frame we have created is our best estimate of how much time you will need. Feel free to adjust it based on your style and the needs and interests of your participants. However, it is important not to skip any of the activities as the exploration will have little meaning without the reflection, content, and analysis pieces or vice versa.

- Support everyone's engagement. As you observe what is happening during the hands-on explorations, be sure that everyone is engaged. Look for the participants who are hanging back or being dominated by another group member. Engage them by asking them what they have noticed or suggest a job they could perform for the group.

FACILITATE REFLECTION

These large group conversations involve discussion of and reflection on the group's experiences during their explorations—group experiences provide the opportunity to learn from one another and draw conclusions from a much larger body of evidence. Teachers will have time to process their experiences in the same way they will do it with children, draw conclusions from the work of the whole group, and build an understanding of the power of reflection and collaborative thinking.

PURPOSE

- Connect the explorations to the underlying science concepts and inquiry skills

- Connect the explorations to the teachers' own teaching and children's learning

- Articulate the teachers' current understandings

GUIDANCE

- Listen carefully. You will be learning a lot about teachers' current understandings of the science content and their teaching of science. Note confusions that you will need to address now or follow up on later. Modify your future interactions to respond to teacher needs and interests, just as you would with children.

- Prompt teachers for fuller descriptions and explanations. You will help them expand their understanding as well as learn more about their thinking if you pursue a comment or question before moving on to the next one. Ask, "What happened? What part of the building fell first? Why do you think it did that?"

- Maintain the focus. Keep your ultimate goal in mind—to prepare teachers to use *Building Structures with Young Children* successfully in their classrooms. Each reflective conversation has an instructional purpose and a limited amount of time. Try to manage the time so teachers have an opportunity to discuss all of the important reflection questions.

PRESENT CONTENT

This strategy is your opportunity to formally share content. The content will be about science concepts and inquiry skills, specifics about *Building Structures with Young Children* and its approach, or descriptions of the teacher's roles. Presentations are supported by overheads and references to sections of the teacher's guide.

PURPOSE

- Begin to understand the *Building Structures with Young Children* approach to science teaching and learning

- Become familiar with the teacher's guide and the many resources it contains

GUIDANCE

- Use the visual and print material that support these presentations. The references to the teacher's guide are important resources for your participants. By referring to them in your presentations, you help participants learn when and how to use them. The overheads will also help your visual learners stay engaged throughout the presentations.

- Make connections between the content of the presentations and the teachers' past teaching or building experiences (for example, when you are talking about observing children's explorations, ask teachers which strategies they have successfully used in the past to document observations). When these connections are explicit it will be easier for participants to absorb the content.

GUIDE ANALYSIS

While the explorations and presentations are important, they will only have an impact on practice when teachers can make connections between what they are learning and their work as teachers. To help them make these connections, engage them in analyzing classroom documentation (such as the video vignettes, children's work samples, teachers' journal entries, and photographs).

PURPOSE

- Connect science content and science teaching to daily work with young children

- Build skill as reflective analytical thinkers

- Learn to see the science ideas and inquiry skills in the many forms of children's communication

- Build the ability to use documentation when assessing individual science teaching as well as the children's science learning

GUIDANCE

- Familiarize yourself with the criteria in this guide that are being used to analyze each document or vignette. For example, you will want to review the content that is important for the analysis of each video vignette before looking at the tape. If you are going to be looking at children's inquiry, review the inquiry diagram and inquiry skills outcomes.

- Begin with description and move to analysis. Good analysis is built on clear ideas about what is being analyzed. Begin these conversations with a description of the documentation—observations of the behaviors and interactions on a video vignette or descriptions of the elements of a child's work sample or of the buildings they built. Ask guiding questions to help participants describe their observations, and then help them make connections to the criteria being used for analysis. For example, describing the parts of a building represented in a child's drawing helps teachers to think about what the child has and hasn't noticed. Then, the teacher can think about what this means. Specifically, they can ask themselves, "Now that I have a better understanding of what this child knows, what does that mean for my next steps as a teacher?"

- Monitor small group conversations. When teachers are working in small groups, listen to the conversations around the room. You will get insight into groups' thinking and can troubleshoot with those groups that get off track. Interject a comment or a question to move a group forward or sit down and facilitate their conversation for a while.

- Remember the science content and inquiry skills. Each classroom artifact or video vignette provides another opportunity for insight into the science content. As teachers see the science concepts reflected in various ways on video or in children's work samples, they will deepen their understanding of these science concepts and the inquiry process.

USING THE VIDEO VIGNETTES

Video vignettes have a special role in "Building Structures with Young Children" training. They provide a unique opportunity for teachers to see the science teaching and learning of other early childhood classrooms. While doing this, teachers begin to think analytically, connecting what they have learned about the *Building Structures with Young Children* approach to actual classroom work.

The teachers shown in these vignettes are at different stages of development as science teachers and vary in their teaching style. They all use important strategies and engage their children in an exploration of building structures, but they all miss opportunities as well. Use these vignettes to draw out important aspects of science teaching and learning, and to identify other approaches that would also be effective. The point is not to criticize or defend the teachers, but to use their work as a stimulus for talking about science teaching and learning.

Many of the children in some of these vignettes are English language learners. Their teacher is using strategies that are particularly effective in helping them communicate their experiences and ideas while learning English. You will find references to these strategies in the instructions so, when relevant, they can be highlighted with teachers.

Each vignette has been selected for a particular purpose, but also presents an opportunity to think about the science concepts in a classroom setting. Use questions that draw out the science present in the video in addition to the other things you want your participants to see—"What science was being explored here?" Reinforce the link between the teaching and the learning—"Why do you think the teacher did that? What did the children gain? How did it focus children's thinking on a science idea? How did it promote inquiry?" Also ask for specifics. Return to the video to show segments again to be sure everyone agrees—"Where did you see evidence of that? What was the child doing? What was the teacher doing?"

Use the vignettes more than once. There is a lot to see and think about and teachers will benefit from multiple viewings. Use them in guided discussions, or allow teachers to take them home or look at them with their colleagues. Provide guiding questions that give focus to the viewing. Use the vignette log that follows to plan ways of using each vignette so that it meets teachers' needs.

Video Vignette Log

The workshop instructions provide additional information about each of these vignettes, including the following: key science concepts being explored, inquiry skills being used, and teacher strategies. The workshops also provide guidance for discussing the vignettes. If you are using a vignette with individual teachers or as part of a guided discussion, be sure to review relevant sections about the vignettes in the workshops and sessions in which they are used.

1. **INTRODUCTION** (7 minutes 18 seconds)

   This montage presents a view of the culture of inquiry in classrooms where the children are engaged in a building structures exploration. Children build with varied materials, pursue questions about stability and balance, and think about what their experiences tell them. Teachers observe children, identify their question, facilitate their inquiry, and document what children say and do. Such snapshots illustrate what children's in-depth, inquiry-based exploration of building structures looks like and the teacher's role as a guide. This montage, which serves as an excellent introduction to *Building Structures with Young Children*, is used in the first basic workshop, and the first advanced workshop, "Creating a Culture of Inquiry." It might also be used for introducing families and community groups to "Building Structures with Young Children."

2. **HAWAIIAN HOUSES** (5 minutes 5 seconds)

   This vignette, filmed in a Boston kindergarten class, shows four girls building in the block area. All kinds of play are evident: constructive, dramatic, symbolic, and exploratory. The teacher's presence is encouraging and she finds an opportunity to connect their work to the science concepts.

   This vignette is used in basic workshop 2, "Getting Ready." It might also be used to

   - Practice observing children's engagement and analyzing their understandings

   - Have a more in-depth discussion of the teacher's role in promoting children's science inquiry, by considering the next steps she might take

3. **OPEN EXPLORATION WITH UNIT BLOCKS** (5 minutes 3 seconds)

   This vignette, filmed in a Boston Head Start classroom, shows a group of five preschool children and their teacher in the block area. Four of these children are English language learners. The teacher encourages this building with questions, comments, and help. She helps them make space, learn appropriate ways to collaborate, and think about the parts of their buildings—roofs, floors, and shapes of the blocks—triangle, cylinder. They count two towers and five of something else.

This vignette is used in basic workshop 3, "Overview of Open Exploration" and advanced workshop 4, "Assessing Children's Science Learning." It might also be used to

- Engage in a deeper analysis of the teacher's role, asking, How might this teacher bring the science forward? What would next steps be for these children's inquiry?

4. FOCUSED EXPLORATION WITH KAPLA BLOCKS (4 minutes 38 seconds)

This vignette, filmed in a Boston kindergarten, shows two preschool children engaged in a focused exploration. They are attempting to replicate an enclosure in a photograph in a Kapla book. The teacher provides support with questions that focus them on identifying the feature of the structure that is key to successfully building up.

This vignette is used in basic workshop 5, "Overview of Focused Exploration." It might also be used to

- Practice observation of children with varying abilities and understandings

- Have a more in-depth discussion of the teacher's role in promoting children's science inquiry and how it reflects strategies discussed in "The Teacher's Role" that appears in the teacher's guide

- Consider next steps the teacher might take and how their investigation of enclosures might proceed

5. BUILDING ENCLOSURES (4 minutes 43 seconds)

In this vignette (from the same classroom as vignette 3), three preschool children are engaged in a focused exploration of enclosures. They are all working with Kaplas. The teacher encourages them to look closely at their structures and compare them, and challenges them to create open space inside.

This vignette is used in advanced workshop 2, "Deepening Children's Science Understandings." It might also be used to

- Consider how the vignette exemplifies focused exploration or strategies suggested in "The Teacher's Role."

6. ENCOURAGING REPRESENTATION (5 minutes 8 seconds)

In this vignette, two children are working at a table, building and drawing. A third child is drawing in the block area. The teacher interacts with them, eliciting comparison of their buildings and their representations. She encourages one child who is representing for the first time.

This vignette is used in advanced workshop 5, "Encouraging Representation." It might also be used to

- Practice observation of children with varying abilities and understandings

- Discuss ways teachers can use children's work as teaching tools

7. TALKING ABOUT DRAWINGS OF BUILDINGS (4 minutes)

In this vignette, two children are drawing their buildings in the block area. Thalia and Roney are both English language learners. The teacher engages them in conversations about their work. The teacher is helping them learn to communicate about their buildings and drawings and heighten their awareness of how they have represented different parts of their buildings.

This vignette is used in advanced workshop 6, "Using Children's Representations as Teaching Tools." The vignette might also be used to

- Discuss children's science understandings, language development, and representation abilities

- Think about what the next steps might be for these children

8. CONSTRUCTING A WALL (2 minutes 49 seconds)

This vignette shows a teacher encouraging Eddie to help Dierdre with a building problem. The teacher helps by articulating the problem and encouraging Eddie to "use his words" as he shares his building strategy.

This vignette is used, along with vignette 9, in advanced workshop 7, "Facilitating Science Talks." The vignette might also be used to discuss strategies for deepening children's science understandings during a focused exploration of enclosures.

9. Group Sharing (4 minutes 56 seconds)

In this vignette, a teacher is facilitating a large group science talk. They are sharing recent building experiences. The teacher uses documents and demonstration to support the engagement of these English language learners. The teacher is anxious not to drag the meeting on too long, but the children keep extending it.

This vignette is used in advanced workshop 7, "Facilitating Science Talks." The vignette might also be used to discuss strategies for helping second language learners communicate their observations and ideas.

GUIDED DISCUSSION PLANS: SAMPLE 1

This beginning-level discussion, which focuses on understanding the *Building Structures with Young Children* teacher's guide, might be used with teachers who have only participated in the basic workshops. Others like it might follow and focus on other aspects of the teacher's guide.

OBJECTIVES

To better understand the open exploration section of the teacher's guide, discuss the following:
- What is the purpose of open exploration, and what does the children's activity look like?
- What does the teacher do during open exploration?

CONTENT

Ask teachers to read the open exploration section of the guide. Begin the meeting by listing key points about open exploration with the teachers.

DOCUMENT MATERIALS

Video cued to vignette 3 or a video created in one of your classrooms.

SAMPLE DISCUSSION QUESTIONS

Describe: What did you see in this video? How would you describe the children's engagement? What about the teacher's actions?

Analyze: Why do you think the teacher responded in a particular way? How does it exemplify open exploration? What other connections can you see between the video and our list?

Prompt: Can you explain what you mean? Why do you think the teacher did that? How does it encourage inquiry? Or, what is the connection there?

Conclude: What does this mean for your teaching? What do you think you will do differently next week? Why? What do you want to accomplish with your students? How will you do that? How will you know when you have accomplished that? What evidence will you look for?

Guided Discussion Plans: Sample 2

A discussion, like this one, that highlights a particular aspect of children's learning, can happen at any time. It builds on a teacher's understanding after the basic or advanced workshops, providing new insight through analysis of a new stimulus or by reviewing a stimulus they are familiar with from a new perspective.

Objectives

To better understand inquiry and what it looks like when children are building structures.

- What is inquiry?
- What aspects of inquiry are three-, four-, or five-year-olds capable of engaging in?
- How does a teacher help children engage in inquiry?

Content

Use the inquiry diagram and description from the teacher's guide. Review key points, writing them on a chart at the beginning of the meeting.

Document Materials

Excerpts from a teacher's journal (p. 10 in the teacher's guide), video cued to vignettes 5 or 8, or a video vignette or series of photographs from one of your classrooms

Sample Discussion Questions

Describe: What exactly did you see the children doing in this video vignette?

Probe: Help them focus on a particular child by asking questions like, "And what was Juan doing?" Be sure they stick to describing the behavior, not analyzing the inquiry.

Analyze: So which inquiry skills were being used? Which science ideas were being explored?

Prompt: Can you explain why you think so? What did the teacher do to encourage Erin? Why do you think she did that? How do you think that influenced Erin's thinking? What evidence was there of that? What understandings about science were evident? Where?

Conclude: What does this mean for your teaching? What do you think you will do differently next week? Why? What do you want to accomplish with your children? How will you do that? How will you know that you have succeeded?

GUIDED DISCUSSION PLANS: SAMPLE 3

This discussion, which could span several meetings, helps teachers connect their teaching to children's learning. It should come after the teachers are well grounded in the *Building Structures with Young Children* approach and are refining their science teaching.

OBJECTIVES

To better understand how children use representation to reflect their science ideas.
- Recognize children's science ideas in representations where they have used various media.
- Select appropriate media, considering topic and children's diverse abilities.
- Use assessment of children's work to plan the next steps.

CONTENT

Important ideas, video vignettes, and work samples from the two advanced workshops on representation.

DOCUMENT MATERIALS

Selected samples of children's work using different media from your classrooms or from workshops.

SAMPLE DISCUSSION QUESTIONS

Describe: Talk about samples one at a time. What do you see in this drawing? What characteristics of the building has Mary illustrated?

Prompt: How has she used shape to represent blocks? Which parts of the building has she represented? Repeat for several samples, varying child ability or media.

Analyze children's work: How do these samples differ?

Prompt: What is the evidence for how they differ?

Analyze teaching: Do these media help children communicate their ideas? What other media might be used with these children? How might you use this document in the classroom?

Prompt: Have you tried that media? Why do you think it will work here? What specifically would you do? What response would you hope for?

Conclude: What does this mean for your teaching? What do you think you will do differently next week? Why? What do you want to accomplish with the children? How will you do that?

GUIDED DISCUSSION PLANNING FORM

Name: _____

Date: _____

Goal: _____

Objective(s): _____

Pre-reading: _____

Content Focus: _____

Stimulus: _____

Questions that encourage description:

Questions that stimulate analysis:

Concluding questions:

Your reflection on the discussion:

GUIDED DISCUSSION PLANNING FORM (CONT'D)

1. Describe the engagement of the teachers in this discussion. What insights did they share as they analyzed the stimulus material? What do they understand? What are their questions?

2. How would you evaluate the effectiveness of the discussion? Consider the appropriateness of the goal, objective(s), materials, and questions. What worked? What would you do differently next time?

3. What are appropriate next steps for these teachers? Do they need more time on this topic or are they ready for a new one? If you are moving to a new one, what will it be? Have the teachers given input into this decision? How might you involve them? Is there potential leadership emerging? How will you nurture it?

Assessing Teacher Growth

Taking time periodically to assess teachers' growth will help you respond to their professional development interests and needs. Assessment will be especially helpful when you are moving from the basic to advanced workshops and when you are planning mentoring or guided discussions. Use the following two tools:

- Science Teacher Development Stages—Describes knowledge and skills at three stages of development as inquiry-based science teachers. Professional development goals are suggested for each stage. Refer to these stages when you have assessment data and want to plan appropriate next steps.

- Evaluating Science Teaching—A tool for recording your observations of teacher practice. Use it to gather evidence on which to base decisions about the next steps in professional development. Planning advanced workshops, guided discussions, and mentoring are all times when this information will be helpful. You might also want to use it to chart teachers' progress, adding evidence as teachers develop new skills. You will find some additional guidance on using this form at the end of the section on science teacher development stages.

SCIENCE TEACHER DEVELOPMENT STAGES

Teachers will go through a developmental process as they learn to use *Building Structures with Young Children*. This process can be defined in three stages: beginning, developing, and refining. Most teachers will likely start as beginners because they have very little experience facilitating an in-depth study of science with young children. Both the content and process of this type of science teaching will be new to them. While the approach to teaching science is new, it is assumed that they have a base in child development and developmentally appropriate practices that will inform their work as science teachers.

Understanding your teachers' current knowledge and skills will help you plan appropriate professional development and set realistic goals with individual teachers, as they will progress through these stages at different rates.

THE TEACHER BEGINNING TO USE *BUILDING STRUCTURES WITH YOUNG CHILDREN*

- Current Knowledge and Skills—The beginning teacher is unfamiliar with many of the approaches used in *Building Structures with Young Children*. If she has experience in teaching science at all it may be setting up a science table, conducting isolated activities, or implementing themes that are rotated on a weekly or biweekly basis.

- Appropriate Goals for Teachers Beginning to Use *Building Structures with Young Children*—Teachers beginning to use *Building Structures with Young Children* will focus on following the step-by-step instructions in the curriculum guides. Possible goals include the following:

  - Beginning to understand the purpose, flow, and activities in the teacher's guide

  - Gaining a basic understanding of the science concepts being explored and the role of inquiry in science teaching and learning

  - Creating the environment as described in the teacher's guide, including materials, sufficient time, and space

  - Engaging children in the exploration and supporting their inquiry

  - Beginning to document children's science experiences

THE TEACHER DEVELOPING HER SCIENCE PRACTICE

- Current Knowledge and Skills—The developing teacher may still struggle with some of the same things the beginning teacher is experiencing, for example, how to get all of the children engaged. But she understands the goals, values the approach, and has some ability to engage children in inquiry-based science. Science engagement will be evident in the environment and interactions in this classroom. The children's interactions and the classroom displays will reveal a focus on building structures. The developing teacher acknowledges children's science explorations and creates opportunities for children to reflect on experiences and ideas through discussion and representation.

- Appropriate Goals—The developing teacher is beginning to focus on improving her science teaching and promoting children's science learning. Possible goals include the following:

    – Continuing to build understanding of the purpose, flow, and activities in the teacher's guide

    – Building a deeper understanding of the science concepts and how young children build their theories and ideas

    – Creating a more "science rich" environment, including displays and accessible books that inform and stimulate investigation

    – Developing the ability to facilitate children's inquiry, balancing exploration with conversation and representation

    – Learning to use teacher's and children's documentation to stimulate inquiry and to connect children's day-to-day science activities

    – Learning to observe, document, and assess children's science engagement and learning

THE TEACHER REFINING HER SCIENCE PRACTICE

- Current Knowledge and Skills—The refining teacher continues to develop her skills and abilities in all of the areas of the developing teacher and may still struggle with some of the same issues. For example, facilitating science talks that are focused on science experiences and ideas or understanding the science more deeply might continue to be challenging. But this teacher is comfortable with her use of the curriculum, the science concepts, and many of the teaching strategies. She uses documentation and reflection to guide her own development. She adapts her teaching, which is based on her understandings of the responses and needs of individual children as well as the whole group. Evidence of young builders' work permeates the classroom. The environment has many examples of children's work; building materials of various sizes, textures, and shapes; and opportunities for small and large group science talks.

- Appropriate Goals—This teacher is focused on building the link between her teaching and the children's science learning. Possible goals include the following:

    – Using all parts of the teacher's guide to develop a system for observation, documentation, assessment, and planning

    – Building a deeper understanding of the science concepts being explored and how children's understanding is expressed in their behaviors and comments

    – Creating an environment that reflects children's current investigations

    – Developing the ability to deepen science thinking through interactions with children

    – Using documents more effectively to encourage children's reflection and further investigations

    – Integrating *Building Structures with Young Children* with math, language, literacy, and social goals

    – Describing children's science engagement and learning to families and others

    – Extending the exploration beyond the teacher's guide or developing explorations of new topics

EVALUATING SCIENCE TEACHING

On p. 207 you will find a tool to guide your evaluation of teachers. Use it when conducting observations of each teacher to determine appropriate professional development and set goals for individual work. You might also want to use it to chart teachers' progress, adding evidence as teachers develop new skills. An observation is unlikely to provide all of the information you need to complete the evaluation. Arrange for a conference with the teacher and discuss what you have observed and some of the things you have not seen, for example, her observational notes or her work with her assistant or volunteers.

Different sections of the form are relevant for evaluating teachers at each stage of development. As teachers become more skilled you will want to expand the aspects of their practice that you are focusing on. Use the following guidance when planning your observations:

- When evaluating beginning teachers, focus on sections I A, B, and C; II A 1 and 2; II B 1.

- When evaluating developing teachers, continue to focus on the sections that you used for the beginning teacher and add sections I D and the rest of II.

- When evaluating refining teachers, use the whole form.

EVALUATING SCIENCE TEACHING

Name: _____

Teacher(s): _____

Date: _____

Observer: _____

Teacher

Behaviors	Evidence
A. Teacher uses *Building Structures* teacher's guide to structure and sequence meaningful science explorations	
1. Follows steps in teacher's guide, using the teaching cycle of engage, explore, and reflect.	
B. Teacher uses environment to stimulate science exploration	
1. Provides materials and tools for explorations as described in *Building Structures* teacher's guide.	
2. Provides variety of two- and three-dimensional representational materials.	
3. Displays materials and books for easy access by children.	
4. Arranges furniture so children have enough room to work in open areas and on tables in groups of three to five.	
5. Creates displays at children's eye level that provide valuable information, relate to current science interests, and show children's own work.	
6. Provides choice times (thirty to forty-five minutes) with opportunities for children to engage with the science materials.	

Behaviors	Evidence
C. Teacher gives attention and positive encouragement to help children focus on science explorations	
1. Uses comments and questions to acknowledge activity and elicit ideas. Listens with genuine interest.	
2. Engages with children, modeling curiosity, play behavior, and use of tools. Invites reluctant explorers to play and helps them manage frustration by engaging them in problem solving.	
D. Teacher uses strategies that deepen children's science understanding and engage them in inquiry	
1. Encourages children's inquiry—observation, questioning, data collection, recording, and analysis. Offers new challenges as children are ready.	
2. Provides materials in varied media for children to represent an aspect of their experience or a developing theory and encourages the children to represent.	
3. Finds ways to focus children on science in their play.	
4. Facilitates science talks in which children share their experiences, ideas, theories, and conclusions.	
E. Teacher systematically observes and documents for assessment and teaching purposes	
1. Documents observations and interactions using various media, such as observation records, photos, audiotape and videotape, and collected work samples.	
2. Uses documents as teaching tools to connect day-to-day activities, stimulate and bring thinking forward, and launch new challenges.	

Children

Behaviors	Evidence
A. Children are engaged	
1. Use materials to gain basic understandings of characteristics and how these characteristics affect buildings. Use materials and designs to create strong structures.	
2. Talk to each other and the adults about their science explorations.	
3. Engage in inquiry: observing, questioning, collecting data, recording, reflecting, and constructing explanations.	
4. Represent a part of their explorations—drawing, using collage materials or clay, or using their bodies to represent their work and scientific knowledge.	
5. Use resources (peers, books, Web sites, and so on) to extend their explorations and gain new information.	
B. Children are motivated and persistent	
1. Are eager to use the areas of the classroom that are designed for science explorations.	
2. Bring in items or tell stories from home that relate to their explorations.	
3. Show enthusiasm and interest extending to lunch table conversation, request reading from books and for dramatic play, and so on.	

Going Deeper

Behaviors	Evidence
A. Teacher helps other adults learn how to support children's science explorations	
1. Supports assistant(s) in developing their ability to encourage children's science explorations.	
2. Finds specific roles for classroom volunteers that support children's science explorations.	
3. When opportunities arise, serves as a mentor to beginning science teachers.	
B. Teacher extends own understanding of science and expands classroom applications	
1. Extends this exploration beyond the steps in the teacher's guide.	
2. Develops explorations of new topics.	
3. Teacher seeks out deeper understanding of science content.	

SCIENCE TEACHER OBSERVATION SYNTHESIS

Teacher: _____

Date: _____

Current goal/objective of teacher: _____

Teacher's goals for science and inquiry in observed activity

Children's Behavior/Comments	Teacher's Response

Questions or points to consider with teacher

SCIENCE TEACHER DEVELOPMENT PLAN

Teacher: _____

Date: _____

Strengths as a science teacher:

One goal for growth as a science teacher:

Objectives:

Activity	Time Frame	Resources Needed

Follow-up: (what and when)

References

SCIENCE AND TEACHING RESOURCES FOR INSTRUCTORS

See resource list for teachers below for additional titles. Note that the teacher resources are also valuable for instructors, and instructors should read all readings before giving them to teachers. You might also want to share some of these instructor resources with teachers.

Bowman, Barbara, ed. 2000. *Eager to learn: Educating our preschoolers.* Washington, D.C.: National Academy Press.

DeVries, R., et al. 2002. *Developing constructivist early childhood curriculum.* New York: Teachers College Press.

Gallas, Karen. 1995. *Talking their way into science.* New York: Teachers College Press.

Goldhaber, Jeanne, and Dee Smith. 1997. You look at things differently: The role of documentation in the professional development of a campus child care center staff. *Early Childhood Education Journal* 25 (1): 3–10.

Harlen, W. 2001. *Primary science: Taking the plunge.* Portsmouth, N.H.: Heinemann.

Landry, Christopher E., and George E. Forman. 1999. Research on early science education. In *The early childhood curriculum: Current findings in theory and practice.* New York: Teachers College Press.

Lind, Karen. 1996. *Exploring science in early childhood: A developmental approach.* 2d ed. Albany, N.Y.: Delmar Publishers.

Lindfors, Judith W. 1999. *Children's inquiry: Using language to make sense of the world.* New York: Teachers College Press.

Moriarty, Robin F. 2002. Helping teachers develop as facilitators of three- to five-year-olds' science inquiry. Entries from a staff developer's journal. *Young Children* 57 (5): 20–24.

Osborne, Roger, and Peter Freyberg. 1985. *Learning in science: The implications of children's science.* Portsmouth, N.H.: Heinemann.

Perry, Gail, and Mary Rivkin. 1992. Teachers and science. *Young Children* 47 (4): 9–16.

Project 2061—Science for All Americans. 1999. *Dialogue on early childhood science, mathematics, and technology education.* Washington, D.C.: American Association for the Advancement of Science.

Schweinhart, Larry J., and David P. Weikart. 1998. Why curriculum matters in early childhood education. *Educational Leadership* 55 (6): 57–60.

Wasserman, Selma, and J. W. George Ivany. 1996. *Who's afraid of spiders? The new teaching elementary science.* 2d ed. New York: Teachers College Press.

SCIENCE AND TEACHING RESOURCES FOR TEACHERS

Cadwell, Louise B., and Brenda V. Fyfe. 1997. Conversations with children. In *First steps toward teaching the Reggio way,* edited by J. Hendrick. Upper Saddle River, N.J.: Merrill/Prentice Hall.

Chaille, Christine, and Lory Britain. 2003. *The young child as scientist: A constructivist approach to early childhood science education.* New York: Allyn & Bacon.

Chalufour, Ingrid, Cindy Hoisington, Robin Moriarty, Jeff Winokurs, and Karen Worth. 2004. The science and mathematics of building structures. *Science and Children* 41 (4).

Copley, Juanita V. 2000. *The young child and mathematics.* Washington, D.C.: National Association for the Education of Young Children (NAEYC).

Doris, Ellen. 1991. *Doing what scientists do: Children learn to investigate their world.* Portsmouth, N.H.: Heinemann.

Feynman, Richard P. 1988. The making of a scientist. In *What do you care what other people think?* New York: W.W. Norton.

Forman, George. 1996. A child constructs an understanding of a water wheel in five media. *Childhood Education* 72 (5): 269–273.

———. 1996. Helping children ask good questions. In *The wonder of it,* edited by B. Neugebauer. Redmond, Wash.: Exchange Press.

———. 1996. Negotiating with art media to deepen learning. *Child Care Information Exchange* 108: 56–58.

Harlan, Jean. 1992. *Science experiences for the early childhood years.* 5th ed. New York: Macmillan Publishing Company.

Hirsch, Elisabeth S., ed. 1996. *The block book.* Washington, D.C.: NAEYC.

Hoisington, Cynthia. 2002. Using photographs to support children's science inquiry. *Young Children* 57 (5): 26–30.

Kostelnik, Marjorie. 1992. Myths associated with developmentally appropriate programs. *Young Children* 47 (4): 17–23.

McIntyre, Margaret. 1984. *Early childhood and science.* Washington, D.C.: National Science Teachers Association.

NAEYC. 1998. Learning to read and write: Developmentally appropriate practices for young children. *Young Children* 53 (4): 30–46.

Osborne, Roger, and Peter Freyberg. 1985. *Learning in science: The implications of children's science.* Portsmouth, N.H.: Heinemann.

Owens, Caroline. 1999. Conversational science 101A: Talking it up! *Young Children* 54 (5): 4–9.

Shepardson, D. P., and S. J. Britsch. 2000. Analyzing children's science journals. *Science and Children* 38 (3): 29–33.

Smith, N. R. 1998. *Observation drawing with children: A framework for teachers.* New York: Teachers College Press.

Sprung, Barbara. 1996. Physics is fun, physics is important, and physics belongs in the early childhood classroom. *Young Children* 51 (5): 29–33.

Tudge, Jonathan, and David Caruso. 1988. Cooperative problem-solving in the classroom: Enhancing young children's cognitive development. *Young Children* 44 (1): 46–52.

Worth, Karen, and Sharon Grollman. 2003. *Worms, shadows, and whirlpools.* Portsmouth, N.H.: Heinemann.

Yinger, J., and S. Blaszka. 1995. A year of journaling—A year of building with young children. *Young Children.* 51 (1): 15–20.

index